D0831155

700040816684

BAKE
YOUR OWN

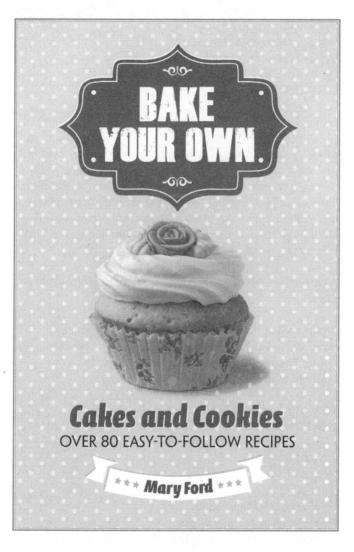

BAKE YOUR OWN

Cakes and Cookies

OVER 80 EASY-TO-FOLLOW RECIPES

★★★ **Mary Ford** ★★★

Michael O'Mara Books Limited

First published in Great Britain in 2013 by
Michael O'Mara Books Limited
9 Lion Yard
Tremadoc Road
London SW4 7NQ

A CIP catalogue record for this book is available from the British
Library.

Papers used by Michael O'Mara Books Limited are natural,
recyclable products made from wood grown in sustainable
forests. The manufacturing processes conform to the
environmental regulations of the country of origin.

ISBN: 978-1-78243-107-7 in hardback print format
ISBN: 978-1-78243-168-8 in ebook format

1 2 3 4 5 6 7 8 9 10

Illustrations by Aubrey Smith
Cover design by Ana Bjezancevic
Designed and typeset by K.DESIGN, Winscombe, Somerset

Printed and bound by CPI Group (UK) Ltd, Croydon CR0 4YY

www.mombooks.com

CONTENTS

CONVERSION TABLES

Conversions are approximate. Ensure you follow only one set of measurements, either metric or imperial, per recipe.

Weight

Metric	Imperial
15 g	½ oz
25 g	1 oz
40 g	1½ oz
50 g	2 oz
85 g	3 oz
115 g	4 oz
145 g	5 oz
175 g	6 oz
200 g	7 oz
225 g	8 oz
250 g	9 oz
285 g	10 oz

Metric	Imperial
350 g	12 oz
375 g	13 oz
400 g	14 oz
425 g	15 oz
450 g	1 lb
550 g	1¼ lb
675 g	1½ lb
750 g	1¾ lb
900 g	2 lb
1.3 kg	3 lb
1.8 kg	4 lb
2.25 kg	5 lb

~ Measurements ~

Metric	Imperial
5 mm	¼ inch
1 cm	½ inch
2.5 cm	1 inch
5 cm	2 inch
7.5 cm	3 inch
10 cm	4 inch
12.5 cm	5 inch
15 cm	6 inch
18 cm	7 inch
20 cm	8 inch
23 cm	9 inch
25 cm	10 inch
30 cm	12 inch

∽ Oven Temperatures ∽

Celsius	Fan Assisted	Fahrenheit	Gas
110°C	Fan 90°C	225°F	Gas ¼
120°C	Fan 100°C	250°F	Gas ½
140°C	Fan 120°C	275°F	Gas 1
150°C	Fan 130°C	300°F	Gas 2
160°C	Fan 140°C	325°F	Gas 3
180°C	Fan 160°C	350°F	Gas 4
190°C	Fan 170°C	375°F	Gas 5
200°C	Fan 180°C	400°F	Gas 6
220°C	Fan 200°C	425°F	Gas 7
230°C	Fan 210°C	450°F	Gas 8
240°C	Fan 220°C	475°F	Gas 9

~ Liquids ~

Metric	Imperial
15 ml	½ fl oz
25 ml	1 fl oz
50 ml	2 fl oz
75 ml	3 fl oz
100 ml	3½ fl oz
125 ml	4 fl oz
150 ml	5 fl oz/¼ pint
175 ml	6 fl oz
200 ml	7 fl oz
225 ml	8 fl oz
250 ml	9 fl oz
300 ml	10 fl oz/½ pint
350 ml	12 fl oz
400 ml	14 fl oz
450 ml	16 fl oz/¾ pint
500 ml	18 fl oz

Metric	Imperial
568 ml	20 fl oz/1 pint
600 ml	1 pint milk
700 ml	1¼ pints
850 ml	1½ pints
1 litre	1¾ pints
1.2 litres	2 pints
1.3 litres	2¼ pints
1.4 litres	2½ pints
1.5 litres	2¾ pints
1.7 litres	3 pints
1.8 litres	3¼ pints
2 litres	3½ pints
2.5 litres	4½ pints
2.8 litres	5 pints
3 litres	5¼ pints

ᵔᵎᵔ US Cups ᵔᵎᵔ

¼ cup	60 ml
⅓ cup	70 ml
½ cup	125 ml
⅔ cup	150 ml
¾ cup	175 ml
1 cup	250 ml
1½ cups	375 ml
2 cups	500 ml
3 cups	750 ml
4 cups	1 litre
6 cups	1.5 litres

ᵔᵎᵔ Spoons ᵔᵎᵔ

Metric	Imperial
1.25 ml	¼ teaspoon
2.5 ml	½ teaspoon
5 ml	1 teaspoon
10 ml	2 teaspoons
15 ml	3 teaspoons/1 tablespoon
30 ml	2 tablespoons
45 ml	3 tablespoons
60 ml	4 tablespoons
75 ml	5 tablespoons
90 ml	6 tablespoons

Mary's Tip

All of the recipes in this book were made using a non-fan-assisted oven. If you too are using one, cook your cakes and cookies on the middle shelf as the top of the oven tends to get quite hot. If your oven *is* fan assisted you can put your bakes wherever you fancy as the fan circulates the heat evenly throughout the oven.

But, whatever your oven, it'll always have its peculiarities, so don't worry if you find your bakes take longer than the recipe suggests. The best thing to do is to make sure you get to know it before commencing.

INTRODUCTION AND TECHNIQUES

~oo~

It's wise to read the information in this chapter before you start baking. Full of invaluable advice on avoiding commonplace baking errors, making sure you have the right ingredients before you start creating and mastering baking techniques, it contains everything you need to know.

~oo~ Introduction ~oo~

Mary Ford enjoyed a long and successful career in baking. What began as an enterprise in teaching cake decorating quickly developed into something much bigger. The absolute highlight of her career came when she was awarded the privilege of creating the wedding cake for Prince Charles and Lady Diana's wedding in 1981.

In this homage to Mary Ford you will find eighty-five of her best recipes to suit a range of occasions. From teatime treats to Christmas delights, *Bake Your Own: Cakes and Cookies* offers you the chance to cater all year round.

Baking is now a more popular pursuit than ever. Capturing the trend for all things home-made, this book gathers together a range of recipes to cater for all tastes and levels of experience. Whether fuelled by a desire to save money and ensure you know what ingredients are going into your family's food, or simply by the fun of baking, you should find everything you need in this collection of recipes.

The focus of this book is on all-time classic bakes, from the reliable Victoria sponge to the more indulgent rich chocolate cake, the nostalgic pineapple upside-down cake to gloriously moreish melting moments. Also included are quick and fun recipes for you to try with any children in your life, and a number of celebratory treats, including Simnel cake and Christmas cookies.

It's time to go forth and bake.

ᴥ Essential Equipment ᴥ

The recipes in this book do not call for any expensive or fancy equipment. But there are some kitchen items that are essential for baking. Most of this equipment is easy to get hold of, relatively cheap to buy and should last you a lifetime.

Scales

An essential item for any baker is a reliable set of scales. Electronic scales are brilliant because they're so precise and convenient to boot. Otherwise old-fashioned scales with weights are also reliable.

Baking Tins

The best sort of cake tins are loose bottomed and non-stick. Regardless of a tin's non-stick properties, always remember to grease and line it before pouring in the mixture (see below).

Each recipe specifies the shape and size of tin needed as using the right tin is crucial for successful baking. If you don't quite have the right size, use a slightly bigger tin and test the cake about five or ten minutes before it's scheduled to be done as they tend to cook more quickly in bigger tins. As a general rule, tins should be two thirds full of mixture.

Never bake in a brand new tin – bake off its shininess in a hot oven and allow to cool before use. Do not rush to get the cake out of the tin once cooked – many cakes are liable to crack if handled too early. The richer the cake, the longer it should be left to cool. Finally, always keep a couple of different-sized baking trays on hand for cookies.

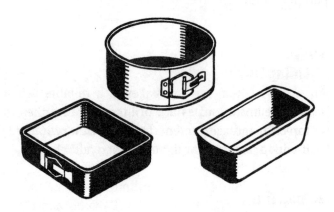

Bowls

If you're a novice baker, a generous-sized mixing bowl with a rounded base should be your first port of call. As you build up your collection you can amass a selection of different sizes of bowls – it's always good to have an extra one or two on standby in case the recipe calls for you to whisk eggs in a separate bowl.

Greaseproof Parchment

Essential for lining cake tins, parchment is sturdier than paper, so always go for this option. Each recipe specifies how you should line the tin, but generally speaking you must grease the tin, lay down the baking parchment then grease the parchment too.

Lining Tins

To base line a round tin, place the sponge tin on top of the greaseproof parchment, draw around it with a pen, cut out the disc and place it in the bottom of the tin.

To line the sides of a round or square tin, cut the greaseproof parchment 5 cm (2 inches) bigger than the depth of the cake tin. You will need 4 pieces for a square tin and 1 piece for round tin. Cover the sides and 2.5 cm (1 inch) around the base with the prepared greaseproof parchment, also ensuring the parchment is 2.5 cm (1 inch) above the tin's height. Fit another piece in the base of the tin.

To line a loaf tin, cut a piece of parchment to fit the length and width of the tin plus approximately 5 cm (2 inch) overhang. Centre the tin on the parchment and make four cuts from the edge to the corners of the tin. Place the parchment inside the tin, overlapping it at the corners.

Measuring Spoons

Cooking shops and department stores showcase an array of attractive and very useful measuring spoons. For the recipes in this book you will need a teaspoon, ½ teaspoon, ¼ teaspoon, a tablespoon and a dessertspoon.

Whisks

Electric whisks are great for convenience and save your wrists. They are also the most effective at mixing ingredients. If you prefer to use a balloon whisk, choose a larger size if whisking eggs. Silicon whisks are good if you're using it in a non-stick pan as it saves the coating.

Spoons

You should use a wooden spoon for general mixing; large metal spoons are essential for folding in egg whites.

Spatula

Great for gathering up any last bits of the cake mix as you spoon it into the tin.

Rolling pin

An essential item when rolling out pastry.

Sieve

Lots of the recipes in this book will call for you to sieve flour in order to weed out any lumps and get lots of air into it. Sieves are also handy when dusting cakes and cookies with icing sugar. Stainless steel sieves are good as they're quite solid and don't, therefore, lose their shape.

Measuring Jug

A transparent heatproof jug is your best option if a recipe calls for measuring liquids.

Wire Tray

Helps to cool cakes and cookies once they've been removed from the tin because they let air circulate beneath.

Pastry Brush

Useful for glazing your pastry with milk or egg; also useful for greasing tins.

Cutters

It's good to keep a range of different shaped and sized cutters for making cookies and scones. Choose metal cutters over plastic, but make sure they're completely dry before storing away – you don't want the metal to rust.

⌐ Ingredients ⌐

All the measurements for the ingredients in this book are given in both metric and imperial. Whichever you choose, stick to one system throughout a recipe – never mix the two.

Assemble all the ingredients and leave them to stand at room temperature for at least an hour before starting to cook to avoid curdling the mixture.

Finally, take care when adjusting the quantities of ingredients; although doubling the ingredients for twice the quantity may work for some cakes, success cannot be guaranteed, so it is best to stick to the amounts given.

Eggs

The recipes in this book tend to call for large size eggs, and always buy free range and organic if you can. Allow eggs to reach room temperature before baking.

Sugar

Careful selection of the type of sugar used can greatly enhance the finished taste and texture of your baked goods. Nutritionally, brown and white sugars are virtually identical, but the distinctive colour and flavour of brown sugar arises from molasses, which is the syrup remaining after all the sugar has been removed from the cane juice. When manufacturing white sugar, the molasses is completely removed whilst the different brown sugars contain more, or less, of the syrup depending on the flavour and colour required. Always make sure you use the sugar specified in the recipe.

Flour

Flour provides structure to your bakes and it's important to use the type stated in the recipe. Self-raising flour is the same as plain flour but with an added leavening agent. If the recipe calls for self-raising flour but you only have plain flour to hand, you can make your own self-raising flour by adding one teaspoon of baking powder to every 110 g of plain flour. Finally, do try to sift flour when you can – it lightens it and ensures an even distribution throughout the mixture.

Fats

Modern-day baking recipes tend to use butter instead of margarine. Butter has a richer flavour, while margarine is lighter and tends to be seen as a little old-fashioned. If you do choose butter, either salted or unsalted is fine to use. Always remove the butter from the fridge ahead of mixing your ingredients otherwise it's a little too hard to mix. If you choose to use margarine, avoid low-fat spreads as they tend to contain a high percentage of water, which makes them unsuitable for baking.

One or two of the recipes in this book call for oil instead of butter. For cakes such as these, make sure you choose an oil that is low in flavour, such as sunflower or groundnut.

Leaveners

Baking powder is commonly added to cake mixtures. It's a mixture of bicarbonate of soda (an alkali) and cream of tartar (an acid), which reacts with the liquid part of cake mixtures to create carbon dioxide. This gas expands during the cooking process, which helps the cake to rise.

Bicarbonate of soda is another raising agent, but it has a slightly bitter taste, so it works better in cakes with stronger flavours.

Whichever leavener the recipe calls for, make sure it hasn't gone out of date as this can affect its usefulness (see page 30).

Cream

The recipes in this book call for double cream – a thick cream that's very easy to whip (and over whip). It contains upwards of 48 per cent fat, so it's fairly indulgent, but that's one of the reasons why it tastes so delicious.

~ひ~ Techniques ~ひ~

Baking is a science and all of the recipes in this book are tried and tested so don't, whatever you do, deviate from the instructions. But if you are a novice baker, the prospect of a new technique can be quite daunting. Do not fear – the methods used in these recipes are very straightforward. If ever in doubt, simply refer to the instructions here for some of the more commonplace techniques.

Sieving

It's a good idea to get into the habit of sifting flour, cocoa powder and icing sugar as this ensures any lumps are removed and also that plenty of air gets into the mixture.

Folding

This helps to keep plenty of air in your mixture when adding flour or whisked egg whites. Use a metal spoon to cut through the middle of the mixture until you reach the bottom of the bowl. Then pull the spoon towards you, lift the mixture and gently fold it back into the middle.

Creaming

This is the method of mixing together the sugar and butter using either a wooden spoon or an electric whisk until the mixture turns light and fluffy. You don't need to use this method if you're making an all-in-one cake.

Separating Eggs

The best tool for separating eggs is the eggshell itself as it cuts through the gloopy white. Over a bowl, crack open the egg so you have two halves of the shell. Hold the egg in one half of the shell and carefully transfer it to the other half. The edge of the shell will cut through the white. Eventually the yolk will be the only thing left in the shell. Once you have this, simply pop it into a separate bowl. Make sure you don't get any yolk in the white as this makes it much more difficult to whisk the egg white.

Whisking Egg Whites

The most important thing to remember when whisking egg whites is that the bowl and whisks are scrupulously clean – a touch of dirt can prevent your whites from reaching peak status.

Melting Chocolate

The best way to melt chocolate is in a glass bowl suspended over a pan of barely simmering water. Heat it carefully – don't let the water touch the bottom of the bowl, be careful not to get any water in the bowl of chocolate and never try to hurry the melting process by turning up the heat. When the chocolate is almost melted, remove from the heat and continue stirring until the chocolate is smooth and completely melted. Keep it warm, stirring occasionally, to prevent it from setting. White chocolate is more likely to separate when it's heated, so keep the heat low. You can also melt chocolate in a microwave on a low setting, but do it in small, 30-second bursts, stirring intermittently.

Making Pastry

You can make pastry either by hand or in a mixing bowl. Make sure all of your ingredients are cold, especially the butter – you want to prevent it from melting before it goes into the oven. And always leave the dough in the fridge for a good half hour before using it.

Making Meringues

When cooking your meringues, open the oven door a few times during the cooking process to let out any moisture. This will help to keep your meringues nice and dry.

～ Baking SOS ～

Your baking problems solved.

How do I prevent the eggs and butter from curdling?

Make sure your ingredients are brought to room temperature before commencing. When you come to cream the butter and sugar, whisk them until the mixture is very pale and has doubled in size – this means you'll have enough air in the mixture to be able to hold the eggs. If you do find the mixture starts to curdle, just add a teaspoon of flour to help bind everything together.

How do I test to see if the cake has cooked?

This is different for each cake. Generally speaking:

* ✮ Placing a fork or a skewer in the centre of a cake works well for dense cakes. When it comes out clean the cake is done.

* ✮ Lightly pressing down on top of the cake to check for springiness works well with lighter cakes such as sponges. If the cake springs back without leaving a dent then the cake is done.

Why hasn't my cake risen?

This could be down to a few different reasons:

* ✮ You might have over-filled the tin with cake mixture. You should aim to leave approximately one third of the tin unfilled to leave sufficient room.

* ✮ The cake might not be ready yet.

* ✮ You might have added too much leavening agent (bicarbonate of soda or baking powder) or it might be out of date, so remember to check the best-before dates before baking.

* ✮ The oven door was opened before the cake was set, so remember to leave the cake be while it's cooking.

How should I store cakes and cookies?

Generally, tins are better than plastic containers for storing cakes and cookies because they're non-porous and won't, therefore, absorb the smells of contents past. Always remember not to keep cakes and biscuits in the same tin – the moisture from the cake will turn the cookies soggy. Cakes also freeze successfully for up to six months.

CAKES

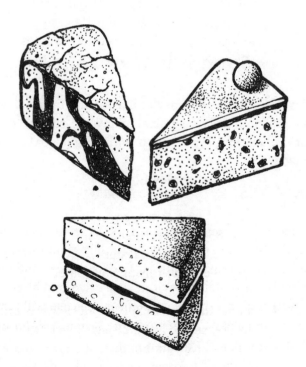

CLASSIC CAKES
~ده~

The time-honoured bakes in this section have graced many a teatime table. Whether in need of a quick and simple Victoria sponge, or something more elaborate, such as a Génoise sponge cake, you will find something to suit every occasion in the recipes that follow.

~ده~ Simple Sponge Cake ~ده~

This versatile cake is easy to master and tastes great, too. For a chocolate sponge, follow the same recipe but replace 15 g (½ oz) flour with 15 g (½ oz) cocoa powder.

Serves 12–16

1½ large eggs
85 g (3 oz) caster sugar
2 tbsp hot water
85 g (3 oz) self-raising flour, sifted

1. Preheat the oven to 200°C/400°F/gas 6 and fully grease and line a 20 cm (8 inch) round sponge tin. Sprinkle sufficient flour into the sponge tin to cover the base and side, then gently shake and turn the tin until all the grease is covered with flour. Tap out any excess.

2. Lightly whisk the egg and pour into the mixing bowl. Add the caster sugar and whisk briskly until the mixture turns thick and creamy. Stir in the hot water.

3. Sprinkle in the sieved flour and gently fold it in with a spatula. Pour the mixture into the prepared tin and place near the top of the oven. When it is finished baking, the cake should be golden brown in colour and should spring back if pressed lightly with fingers. After 14 minutes, open the oven door slowly and check to see if the sponge is cooked. If it is pale in colour, continue baking. Repeat the test every 2–3 minutes until the cake is done.

4. Leave to cool for 5 minutes, then remove from the tin onto greaseproof parchment covered in caster sugar. Upturn the sponge and place on a wire rack until cold.

Mary's Tip
Wrap the cooled sponge in waxed paper and store in an airtight tin. Eat within 3 days, or freeze for up to 6 months and use within 3 days of defrosting.

~⦿~ *Simple Génoise Cake* ~⦿~

Madeleines, the traditional shell-shaped French cakes, are made using a Génoise mixture. This recipe can be easily adapted to make a chocolate Génoise – simply replace 30 g (1 oz) flour with 30 g (1 oz) cocoa powder.

Serves 12–16

85 g (3 oz) butter
85 g (3 oz) margarine
170 g (6 oz) caster sugar
3 large eggs
170 g (6 oz) self-raising flour, sifted

1. Preheat the oven to 190°C/375°F/gas 5 and lightly grease and line a 25 cm (10 in) round tin **or** a 23 cm (9 in) square sponge tin.

2. Beat together the butter and margarine until soft. Beat in the caster sugar until light and fluffy.

3. Crack open the eggs into a separate bowl, then thoroughly beat in the egg a small portion at a time.

4. Gently fold the flour into the creamed mixture, being careful not to over mix. Spoon the mixture into the prepared tin. Bake in the centre of the oven for 20 minutes. When it is finished baking, the cake should be golden brown in colour and should spring back if pressed lightly with a finger. After 20 minutes, open the oven door slowly and draw your fingers across the cake, pressing lightly. If it leaves an indentation, continue baking. Repeat every 2–3 minutes until the cake is done.

5. Leave to cool for 5 minutes, then remove from the tin onto greaseproof parchment covered in caster sugar. Upturn the sponge and place on a wire rack until cold.

Mary's Tip
Wrap the cooled sponge in waxed paper and store in an airtight tin. Eat within 3 days, or freeze for up to 6 months and use within 3 days of defrosting.

‑ⴲ‑ *Carrot Cake* ‑ⴲ‑

A classic cake that's moist, delicious and very easy to make.

Serves 12–16

For the cake:

225 g (8 oz) carrots, grated
170 ml (6 fl oz) corn oil
170 g (6 oz) light brown soft sugar
3 large eggs, whisked
2 tbsp golden syrup
1 tsp vanilla essence
170 g (6 oz) plain flour
1 tsp bicarbonate of soda
1 tsp baking powder
1 tsp cinnamon
½ tsp grated nutmeg
1 tsp salt
115 g (4 oz) walnut pieces, roughly chopped
30 g (1 oz) bran

For the filling and topping:

115 g (4 oz) butter
225 g (8 oz) icing sugar, sifted
115 g (4 oz) low fat soft cream cheese
½ tsp vanilla essence

1. Preheat the oven to 180°C/360°F/gas 4 and grease and line a 21.5 cm (8½ inch) round cake tin.

2. Mix together the carrots, oil, sugar, eggs, golden syrup and vanilla essence until smooth.

3. Sift together the flour, bicarbonate of soda, baking powder, cinnamon, nutmeg and salt. Then mix in the chopped walnuts and bran.

4. Add to the carrot mixture and beat well. Pour the mixture into the tin and bake on the middle shelf for 1¼ hours. Leave in the tin for 5 minutes then turn out onto a wire tray to cool.

5. To make the filling, cream together the butter and the icing sugar until smooth. Beat in the cream cheese and the vanilla essence until light and fluffy.

6. Slice the cake in half and fill the centre with half of the filling. Use the rest to coat the top of the cake. Decorate with pecan nuts or sugar paste carrots.

~ Swiss Roll ~

This all-in-one Swiss roll is quick and easy to make once you've mastered the technique of rolling the hot sponge.

Serves 10–12

For the cake:

85 g (3 oz) butter
170 g (6 oz) caster sugar
3 large eggs
170 g (6 oz) self-raising flour

For the filling:

60 g (2 oz) jam, warmed

1. Preheat the oven to 200°C/390°F/gas 6 and lightly grease and line a 33 × 23 cm (13 × 9 inch) Swiss roll tin.

2. Place all the ingredients into a bowl and beat until light and creamy. Pour the mixture into the tin and spread evenly using a trowel-shaped palette knife. Bake on the middle shelf of the oven for 10–12 minutes.

3. In the meantime, place a moist tea towel onto your worktop, then place a sheet of greaseproof parchment covered with caster sugar on top. Take the sponge out of the

oven and turn immediately onto the sugared parchment.

4. Remove the greaseproof parchment the sponge was baked in, then immediately roll up the sponge in the sugared parchment and leave for 5 minutes to cool. Carefully unroll the sponge and spread the jam filling on the uncovered side. Roll up again, without the sugared parchment or towel, and leave to cool on a wire tray.

Mary's Tip
Waste no time once the sponge is cooked.
If you are slow the edges will go crisp as they cool,
causing the sponge to crack as you roll it.

⊶ *Victoria Sandwich* ⊶

Try experimenting with this all-in-one recipe by adding a few drops of vanilla essence to the mixture before baking.

Serves 12

For the cake:

285 g (10 oz) self-raising flour, sifted
2½ tsp baking powder
285 g (10 oz) butter
285 g (10 oz) caster sugar
5 large eggs

For the filling:

raspberry jam
buttercream (see box)

For the topping:

icing sugar for dusting

1. Preheat the oven to 170°C/340°F/gas 3 and grease and line two 21.5 cm (8½ inch) round sandwich tins.

2. Thoroughly sift the flour and baking powder together. Place all the ingredients into a bowl and mix together thoroughly with an electric whisk on a slow speed, or by hand with a wooden spoon.

3. Divide the mixture equally into the tins and gently spread level. Bake on the middle shelf of the oven for 35–45 minutes. Turn out onto a wire tray to cool. Sandwich together with the jam and then dust the top with icing sugar.

Making Buttercream

The most important rule for buttercream is: the longer you beat it, the lighter it becomes, both in texture and colour.

> 170 g (6 oz) unsalted butter
> 340 g (12 oz) icing sugar, sifted
> 3 tbsp warm water

1. Allow the ingredients to reach room temperature.

2. Beat the butter until light. Gradually add the icing sugar, beating well after each addition. Beat in the water and add any flavour the recipe calls for.

To make chocolate buttercream simply add 1 tsp cocoa powder to the mix.

⊸ *Pineapple* ⊸
Upside-Down Cake

Step back in time with this retro bake.

Serves 8–12

2 tbsp golden syrup
30 g (1 oz) light brown soft sugar
340 g (12 oz) can of pineapple rings
a handful of glacé cherries, cut in half
3 large eggs
85 g (3 oz) caster sugar
85 g (3 oz) plain flour, sifted

1. Preheat the oven to 180°C/360°F/gas 4 and grease and line a 20 cm (8 inch) round sponge tin.

2. Using a pastry brush, coat the greaseproof parchment at the base of the tin with the golden syrup then sprinkle on the brown sugar. Strain the pineapple rings and place alongside each other at the bottom of the tin. Fill each pineapple ring with a glacé cherry.

3. Whisk the eggs and sugar until light and fluffy then gently fold in the flour. Pour the mixture into the tin and bake on the middle shelf for 40–45 minutes.

4. After baking leave in the tin for 15 minutes, upturn and carefully turn out onto a wire tray to cool.

Mary's Tip
Before adding eggs to any cake mixture, always crack them open into a separate, small basin to check for freshness. This way you avoid any bad eggs contaminating the cake.

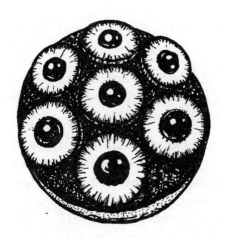

ꞏ◌ꞏ *Madeira Cake* ꞏ◌ꞏ

Traditionally eaten in the nineteenth century with a glass of Madeira wine first thing in the morning, this cake is now widely regarded as a classic teatime treat.

Serves 10

170 g (6 oz) butter
170 g (6 oz) caster sugar
3 large eggs
145 g (5 oz) self-raising flour, sifted
115 g (4 oz) plain flour, sifted
grated rind and juice of 1 orange
30 g (1 oz) cube sugar, crushed
a few strands of crystallized orange peel

1. Preheat the oven to 170°C/325°F/gas 3 and line and grease a 900 g (2 lb) loaf tin.

2. Beat together the butter and the sugar until light and fluffy. Beat in the eggs, one at a time, then fold in the flours.

3. Add the orange rind and juice and stir well. Pour into the prepared tin, and smooth over. Sprinkle with the crushed sugar and a few strands of crystallized orange peel and bake for approximately 1 hour 15 minutes. Turn out onto a wire tray to cool.

~ Génoise Sponge Cake ~

A light and creamy cake that is easier to make than the finished article might suggest. When cutting cold Génoise, twist the knife from left to right; you may find a straight cut produces a crumbly edge.

Serves 16

Please note: this recipe calls for two sponges. The ingredients list below is for a single sponge. If your oven is large enough to accommodate two tins, double the quantities in the mixture. If not, make and bake one at a time.

For one sponge:

45 g (1½ oz) butter, melted
3 large eggs
85 g (3 oz) caster sugar
70 g (2½ oz) plain flour, sifted
1 tbsp cornflour, sifted

For the filling:

seedless raspberry jam
300 ml (10 fl oz) double cream, whipped
icing sugar for dusting
1 glacé cherry

1. Preheat the oven to 180°C/360°F/gas 4 and line and grease a 20 cm (8 inch) round sandwich tin.

2. Melt the butter in a saucepan over a gentle heat, then remove from the heat. Whisk the eggs and sugar in a bowl sitting over a pan of hot water until light and fluffy. Remove the water and continue whisking until the mixture is cool. Sift the flours together and fold half into the mixture of the eggs and sugar. Fold in half the melted butter.

3. Gradually fold in the remaining butter and flour alternately. Pour into the tin and bake on the middle shelf for 25–30 minutes. After baking turn out onto a wire tray to cool.

4. Cut out the centre of one sponge. Spread the jam over the base of the other sponge and place the ring on top. Fill the centre with the whipped cream to form a peak.

5. Cut the circle into equal-sized sections and arrange on top of the cream. Dust lightly with sifted icing sugar and decorate with a glacé cherry.

Mary's Tip

To make a light sponge, slightly warm the flour before mixing it in. Cold flour will chill the eggs, which will release some of the air beaten in. Because air is the only raising agent in a Génoise you should do everything possible to retain as much of it as possible.

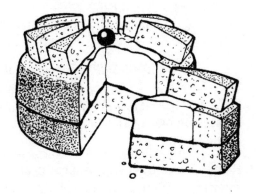

~ஒ~ *Ginger Cake* ~ஒ~

A moist and tangy tasting cake that is perfect
served with afternoon tea.

Serves 16

115 g (4 oz) butter
8 tbsp golden syrup
115 g (4 oz) dark brown soft sugar
225 g (8 oz) plain flour, sifted
a pinch of salt
2 tsp ground ginger
1 tsp bicarbonate of soda
1 large egg
4 tbsp plain yoghurt

1. Preheat the oven to 170°C/340°F/gas 3 and
grease and line an 18.5 cm (7¼ inch) square
sandwich tin.

2. Heat the butter, syrup and sugar in a
saucepan until the butter has fully melted. Do
not let the mixture boil. Remove from heat
and allow to cool.

3. Sift together flour, salt, ginger and
bicarbonate of soda into a bowl. With a
spoon, beat in the warm mixture, the egg and
then the yoghurt to form a smooth batter.

4. Pour the cake mixture into the tin and bake
on a low shelf for 55 minutes. Leave to cool in
the tin, then remove and place on a wire tray.

Mary's Tip
If you intend on keeping the cake for more than
a day or two it will benefit from a buttercream
icing flavoured with 2 tsp lemon juice and a few
pieces of stem or crystallized ginger on top.

CHOCOLATE CAKES
~oɩo~

A perennial favourite, chocolate cake can be served at a variety of celebrations. From afternoon tea to a formal dinner, this versatile but unfailingly delicious cake is guaranteed to go down a treat.

~oɩo~ *Rich Chocolate Cake* ~oɩo~

This cake is a sumptuous, beautifully presented treat, perfect to serve as pudding at a dinner party or as a very grown-up birthday cake.

Serves 16–20

For the cake:

145 g (5 oz) butter
285 g (10 oz) dark brown soft sugar
3 large eggs
2 tbsp black treacle
1 tsp vanilla essence
225 g (8 oz) plain flour, sifted
½ tsp bicarbonate of soda
2 tsp baking powder
a pinch of salt
225 ml (7½ fl oz) milk
60 g (2 oz) plain chocolate, melted

For the filling:

170 g (6 oz) chocolate buttercream (see page 41)

For the fudge icing:

450 g (1 lb)caster sugar
150 ml (¼ pint) milk
115 g (4 oz) butter
2 tbsp golden syrup
1 tsp cocoa powder
60 g (2 oz) plain chocolate

To decorate:

chocolate curls
cocoa powder for dusting

1. Pre-heat the oven to 180°C/360°F/gas 4.
Lightly grease two 20 cm (8 inch) round
sandwich tins.

2. Beat together the butter and sugar.
Thoroughly beat in the egg a little at a time.
Stir in the treacle and the vanilla essence.
Sift together the flour, bicarbonate of soda,
baking powder and salt. Fold into the
creamed mixture.

3. Gradually fold in the melted chocolate and
sufficient milk to turn the mixture into a
thick batter. Divide the mixture between
tins and bake on the middle shelf for 30–35
minutes. Turn out onto a wire tray to cool.

4. To make the fudge icing, place all the
ingredients into a heavy-based saucepan
and heat gently, stirring until the sugar
has melted. Bring to the boil and cook to
116°C/240°F (test with a thermometer) or
until the syrup forms a soft ball that can be
squashed when dropped into cold water
(you will have to conduct a test to find this
out). Remove from the heat and leave to cool
for 10 minutes, then beat it until it is thick
enough to spread.

5. Sandwich the sponges together with buttercream filling. Spread the fudge over the top and sides. Leave until set. Decorate the top of the cake with chocolate curls and then dust with cocoa powder.

Mary's Tip

To make the chocolate curls, simply scrape a vegetable peeler or knife along the flat part of a bar of chocolate. Try to apply an even pressure to ensure you make pretty ringlets. Short scrapes will give you small curls, while a long and steady scrape will give you bigger curls.

~ Chocolate and Orange ~ Cake

Do not be daunted by the list of ingredients. This cake is straightforward to make and tastes delicious. Once you have mastered the cake, why not try experimenting with the chocolate fudge icing (see page 56).

Serves 8–10

For the cake:

115 g (4 oz) butter
115 g (4 oz) caster sugar
grated rind ½ orange
grated rind ½ lemon
60 g (2 oz) drinking chocolate powder
115 g (4 oz) ground almonds
2 large eggs, beaten
60 g (2 oz) self-raising flour, sifted
1 dsp brandy (optional)

For the filling:

5 tbsp jam (apricot, raspberry or lemon curd), boiled

For the icing:

115 g (4 oz) plain or milk chocolate
60 g (2 oz) unsalted butter
1 large egg, beaten
170 g (6 oz) icing sugar, sifted

1. Preheat the oven to 160°C/320°F/gas 2½ and lightly grease and base line a 900 g (2 lb) loaf tin.

2. For the cake, beat together the butter and the sugar until light and fluffy. Mix in the grated orange and lemon rind. Stir in the chocolate powder and ground almonds then beat well again. Whisk the eggs in a separate bowl until well mixed.

3. Beat the eggs into the mixture a little at a time. Add a tablespoon of the flour and brandy, if required. Fold in the remaining flour using a spatula or spoon.

4. Spoon the mixture into the tin and bake on the middle shelf for 45 minutes to 1 hour. After baking leave for 20 minutes then turn out onto a wire tray to cool. Slice in half then fill and coat the outside of the cake with the jam.

5. For the icing, melt the chocolate and the butter together slowly in a small bowl sat on top of a pan of barely simmering water. Stir in the egg. Remove from the heat, then stir in the icing sugar and beat well.

6. When the topping is slightly cooled spread over the top and sides of the cake.

Mary's Tip

Try adding some extra ingredients to the
chocolate fudge icing:
2 tbsp rum; grated rind of 1 orange;
1 tbsp honey instead of 30 g (1 oz) sugar;
1 tsp instant coffee granules; a pinch of ground
ginger plus 2 tbsp chopped stem ginger

∽ Lemon and Chocolate ∽ Marble Cake

The flavour combination of lemon and chocolate works wonderfully in this delicious cake. The finished cake is fairly tall and reveals a wonderful layering effect once cut.

Serves 8–10

340 g (12 oz) plain flour, sifted
a pinch of salt
3 tsp baking powder
130 g (4½ oz) butter
130 g (4½ oz) caster sugar
2 medium-sized eggs
3 tsp grated lemon rind
200 ml (7 fl oz) milk
170 g (6 oz) plain chocolate, finely chopped or grated
icing sugar for dusting

Mary's Tip
Salt is a key ingredient in this cake, as it is in many other recipes. Without salt, cakes can be flavourless. It also makes the gluten in the flour more elastic, thereby helping the mixture to rise.

1. Preheat the oven to 190°C/370°F/gas 5 and grease and base line an 18 cm (7 inch) round cake tin.

2. Sift together the flour, salt and baking powder. Rub in the butter until the mixture resembles breadcrumbs. Add the sugar, eggs, lemon rind and milk and stir the mixture with a wooden spoon until it has a soft dropping consistency.

3. Spoon one third of the mixture into the tin, then sprinkle on some of the grated chocolate. Spoon half the remaining mixture on top, then add more grated chocolate. Spoon the remaining mixture on top then, finally, sprinkle on the remaining grated chocolate.

4. Bake on the middle shelf for 15 minutes, then reduce the heat to 180°C/350°F/gas 4 and continue baking for 1 hour. Leave in the tin for 30 minutes, remove and leave to cool on a wire tray. Dust lightly with icing sugar.

～ Uncooked Chocolate Cake ～

This lunchbox friendly cake is simple to make and tastes delicious.

Serves 16–20

For the base:

115 g (4 oz) sweet biscuits
60 g (2 oz) digestive biscuits
60 g (2 oz) walnuts, roughly chopped
100 g (3½ oz) butter
30 g (1 oz) caster sugar
85 g (3 oz) golden syrup
60 g (2 oz) cocoa powder, sifted

For the topping:

115 g (4 oz) milk chocolate
1 tbsp hot water
60 g (2 oz) butter
170 g (6 oz) icing sugar, sifted

To decorate:

a handful of walnuts
a handful of dark and white chocolate, grated

1. Lightly grease a 20 cm (8 in) flan ring and place onto a flat serving dish or board.

2. Place the biscuits in a plastic bag and roughly crush using a rolling pin. Add the walnuts to the biscuits.

3. In a bowl, cream together the butter, sugar and syrup. Beat in the cocoa powder then mix in the biscuits. Press evenly into the flan ring, cover and leave in the refrigerator overnight.

4. To make the topping, slowly heat the chocolate, water and butter together in a bowl sitting on top of a saucepan of barely simmering water. When melted, beat in the icing sugar. Spread over the top of the cooled base and decorate with walnuts and grated chocolate.

FRUIT AND NUT CAKES

~ⓔⓘⓞ~

This broad selection of recipes encompasses classic bakes, such as a basic fruit cake, to the more adventurous, such as a German apple cake. Whichever cake you choose to make, the hungry hordes are sure to enjoy it.

~ⓔⓘⓞ~ *Basic Fruit Cake* ~ⓔⓘⓞ~

This recipe produces 445 g (1 lb) of finished cake. Double the ingredients (and the size of the cake tin) for a 2 lb cake, and so forth. You will also need to factor in more cooking time, though stick to the same oven temperature for each: allow 1¾ hours for a 2lb cake; 2½ hours for a 3lb cake; 3½ hours for a 4lb cake; 4 hours for a 5lb cake; 4¼ hours for a 6lb cake. And, although it isn't necessary to freeze this fruit cake, it can be done. But a decorated fruit cake should not be frozen unless the almond paste and icing have been removed first.

For the cake:

70 g (2½ oz) currants
70 g (2½ oz) sultanas
30 g (1 oz) raisins
30 g (1 oz) glacé cherries, halved
45 g (1½ oz) mixed peel
peel and juice of ¼ lemon
2 tsp brandy or rum
60 g (2 oz) plain flour, sifted
a pinch salt
a pinch nutmeg
a pinch mixed spice
1 large egg, beaten
60 g (2 oz) butter
60 g (2 oz) brown sugar
20 g (¾ oz) ground almonds

Soaking mixture:

equal quantities of rum, sherry and glycerine (or spirits of your choice): 1 tbsp per 445 g (1 lb) of cake.

1. Preheat the oven to 140°C/275°F/gas 1 and grease and line either a 12 cm (5 inch) round tin, or a 10 cm (4 inch) square tin, approximately 7 cm (3 inches) deep (see page 19).

2. Weigh the ingredients out onto separate sheets of greaseproof parchment, then inspect, wash and dry the fruit. Place the fruit, lemon peel and the liquor into a bowl and mix thoroughly.

3. In a separate bowl, sift together the flour, salt and spices. In a separate, small bowl, crack open the egg. Leave all the ingredients at room temperature for 12 hours.

4. Beat the butter until light, then beat in the sugar until light and fluffy. Thoroughly beat in the egg a small portion at a time. Stir in the ground almonds.

5. Fold the flour and the spices lightly into the mixture and mix until clear, then add the fruit. Add the lemon juice and stir thoroughly but DO NOT BEAT.

6. Pour the mixture into the tin, dip your hand in luke warm water and then flatten the mixture with the back of your hand. Place the cake in centre of the oven, with an ovenproof bowl containing water sitting beneath. Bake for 1¼ hours and remove the bowl of water after 40 minutes. After 1¼ hours insert a steel skewer into the centre of the cake and remove slowly. If it is clean, the cake is ready. If the mixture clings to the skewer, put the cake back in the oven and continue testing every 10 minutes. Once baked, remove from the oven and leave in the tin in a cool place for 24 hours.

7. Carefully remove the greaseproof parchment from the cake, upturn the cake and brush on the soaking mixture. Wrap the cake in waxed paper (and not cling film, tin foil or a sealed plastic container), date it and leave to mature in a cool, dry atmosphere which allows odourless air circulation and with no direct sunlight.

Mary's Tip

A darker fruit cake can be made by substituting 10 per cent of the brown sugar with black treacle.

What Went Wrong?

This helpful list should help you pinpoint any fruit-cake-based troubles:

- ✴ If not stored correctly, the cake can become mouldy. This could be due to various reasons: it was wrapped while still warm; it was wrapped after being out for too long; it was wrapped in inferior quality paper; it was stored in a variable temperature; the cake was under baked; it was soaked with too much alcohol after baking; it was stored in a damp atmosphere.

✸ Too hot an oven will produce a cracked, crusted top and an uncooked centre. In addition the fruit may be burnt and bitter.

✸ Too cool an oven will produce an uncooked cake, which will dry out quickly and have a very thick crust.

✸ If the cake has been baked at the correct temperature but the middle has sunk it could contain either too much liquid in the batter, baking powder, sugar or fat.

✸ If the cake is crumbly, any of the following could be the cause: curdled batter; overbeaten fat, sugar and eggs; under mixing the flour and fruit; too little sugar.

‑ois‑ *Citrus Cake* ‑ois‑

A quick, easy and zesty cake. Improves with freezing.

Serves 8

For the cake:

115 g (4 oz) butter
100 g (3½ oz) caster sugar
2 large eggs
2 tbsp lemon curd
145 g (5 oz) self-raising flour, sifted

For the topping:

2 tbsp granulated sugar dissolved in the juice
of ½ a lemon

1. Preheat the oven to 180°C/360°F/gas 4 and grease and base line a 900 g (2 lb) loaf tin.

2. Place all the ingredients into a mixing bowl and beat until light and fluffy. Be careful not to overbeat.

3. Spoon the mixture into the tin and bake on the middle shelf for 50–55 minutes.

4. When baked, brush immediately with the topping syrup, then leave in the tin until cool. Remove from tin and place onto a wire tray until cold.

~๑๑~ *Rhubarb and Date Cake* ~๑๑~

Pale pink forced rhubarb has a mellower flavour than the robust outdoor variety, but both work well with the sweetness of dates.

Serves 12

170 g (6 oz) plain flour, sifted
½ tsp baking powder
85 g (3 oz) butter
115 g (4 oz) caster sugar
225 g (8 oz) rhubarb, chopped into small cubes
115 g (4 oz) stoned dates, chopped
1 large egg, beaten
4 tbsp milk
icing sugar for dusting

1. Preheat the oven to 190°C/370°F/gas 5 and grease and line a 15 cm (6 inch) round cake tin.

2. Sift the flour and baking powder into a bowl. Rub in the butter to form a fine crumbly texture, then stir in the sugar. Stir the rhubarb and the dates into the mixture. Stir in the beaten egg and milk.

3. Pour the mixture into the tin, level and bake on the middle shelf for 1½–2 hours. After baking, leave for 10 minutes then turn out onto a wire tray to cool. Dust with icing sugar.

✎ *Orange and Seed Cake* ✎

Caraway is a warming spice that works wonderfully with citrusy orange.

Serves 12–16

170 g (6 oz) butter
170 g (6 oz) caster sugar
3 large eggs
1 tbsp caraway seeds
1 tbsp milk
grated rind and juice of 1 orange
225 g (8 oz) plain flour, sifted
1½ level tsp baking powder
icing sugar for dusting

1. Preheat the oven to 170°C/340°F/gas 4 and grease a 21.5 cm (8½ inch) brioche tin.

2. Cream the butter until soft. Add the sugar and beat until light and fluffy, then thoroughly beat in the eggs one at a time.

3. Stir in the seeds, milk and orange rind. Sift together the flour and baking powder and fold into the creamed mixture, alternating with the orange juice.

4. Spoon the mixture into the tin and bake on the middle shelf for 45 minutes. Leave to cool for 5 minutes then turn out onto a wire tray to cool. Dust with icing sugar.

❧ Coconut Cake ❧

A crunchy, buttery cake topped with a sweet and creamy icing – what's not to love?

Serves 10–14

For the cake:

145 g (5 oz) butter
170 g (6 oz) caster sugar
2 large eggs
3 tbsp milk
225 g (8 oz) self-raising flour, sifted
115 g (4 oz) desiccated coconut

For the topping:

115 g (4 oz) cream cheese
30 g (1 oz) butter
170g (6 oz) icing sugar, sifted

To decorate:

a handful of toasted flaked coconut

1. Preheat the oven to 170°C/340°F/gas 3 and grease and base line a 900 g (2 lb) loaf tin.

2. Cream the butter and sugar until light and fluffy. Beat together the egg and milk and add slowly to the creamed butter and sugar, beating well. Slowly fold in the flour and coconut using a metal spoon.

3. Pour the mixture into the tin and bake on the middle shelf for 1½ hours. After baking, leave the cake in the tin to cool. Turn out onto a wire tray when cold.

4. For the topping, beat all the ingredients together until pale and creamy. Spread or pipe onto the top of the cake and sprinkle with toasted coconut.

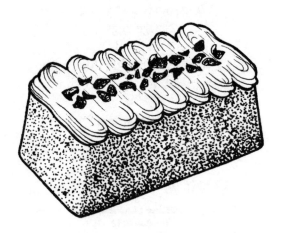

❧ Spicy Plum and ❧ Syrup Cake

The sweetness of the plums is given a little kick with the addition of ground allspice.

Serves 16

For the cake:

440 g (1 lb) self-raising flour, sifted
a pinch of salt
1 tsp allspice
225 g (8 oz) butter, hard
115 g (4 oz) soft light brown sugar
115 g (4 oz) raisins
450 g (1 lb) fresh plums, halved and stones removed
8 tbsp golden syrup
4 large eggs

For the topping:

3 tbsp soft light brown sugar
1 tsp allspice

1. Preheat the oven to 180°C/360°F/gas 4 and grease and fully line a 21.5 cm (8½ in) round cake tin.

2. Sift the flour, salt and allspice into a mixing bowl. Cut the butter into pieces then rub into the flour to form a fine crumbly mix. Stir in the sugar and the raisins.

3. Put aside 10–12 half plums and chop the remaining into small pieces. Beat the syrup and the eggs together then blend into the mixture with the chopped plums.

4. Spoon the mixture into the tin and level. Place the plum halves on top. Mix together the topping ingredients and sprinkle on the top of the cake. Bake on the middle shelf for 1¼ hours. After baking, leave in the tin until cold.

Mary's Tip
Wrap the cake in foil and keep for at least two days before eating.

~ Dundee Cake ~

Traditional Scottish fare, Dundee Cake is one of the most difficult bakes to test for readiness. First warm your skewer by placing it between the cake and the tin as a warm skewer will give a better indication of readiness when you stick it into the centre of the cake. If the skewer comes out quite clean, the cake is ready. If not, test after a further 10–15 minutes.

Serves 8–10

For the cake:

1 tsp bicarbonate of soda
4 tbsp water
115 g (4 oz) butter
200 g (7 oz) caster sugar
115 g (4 oz) dried apricots, chopped
375 g (13 oz) sultanas
4 tbsp dark rum
2 large eggs, beaten
225 g (8 oz) strong plain flour, sifted
2 tsp baking powder
1 tbsp golden syrup
1 heaped tbsp marmalade

For the topping:

60 g (2 oz) blanched almonds, split in half
2 tbsp milk
60 g (1 oz) caster sugar

1. Preheat the oven to 170°/340°F/gas 3 and grease and line a 16.5 cm (6½ inch) round cake tin.

2. Dissolve the bicarbonate of soda in the water, pour into a saucepan and add the butter, sugar and fruits. Bring to the boil on a low heat then simmer for 15 minutes. Remove from heat and leave to cool completely, then add the rum. Beat the eggs until frothy then add to the mixture.

3. Sift the flour and baking powder together then fold into the mixture with the syrup and marmalade, using a metal spoon. Place the almonds into a small bowl and cover with the milk. Leave for two minutes.

4. Spoon the cake mixture into the tin and level. Drain the almonds (but keep aside the milk) and arrange in tight circles around the top of the cake. Sprinkle the top with the milk and then with the caster sugar.

5. Place on the middle shelf and bake for 1¾ hours. Test for readiness by inserting a steel skewer into the centre of the cake and removing slowly. If it is clean, the cake is ready. If the mixture clings to the skewer, reduce the oven temperature to 150°C/300°F/gas 2 and cook until baked. When cooked, leave in the tin for 15 minutes, then turn out onto a wire tray and leave to cool.

Mary's Tip

If you'd prefer the almonds on top to be less well done, remove the cake from the oven half way through cooking and scatter the almonds on, followed quickly with a brush of milk and sugar. Although less neatly arranged, the almonds will come out paler in colour on the finished cake.

~ଚଡ଼ **Walnut Roll** ଚଡ଼~

A dense and rich Swiss roll.

Serves 10–12

For the cake:

90 g (3¼ oz) plain flour
20 g (¾ oz) cocoa powder
½ heaped tsp baking powder
5 large eggs, separated
145 g (5 oz) caster sugar
115 g (4 oz) walnuts, ground
4 dsp hot water

For the filling:

85 g (3 oz) caster sugar
300 ml (½ pint) double cream
a handful of walnuts, chopped
chocolate pieces

Mary's Tip
Chill the cream before whisking and avoid over
whipping. Once the whipped cream is applied to the
cake it is best consumed that day.

1. Preheat the oven to 180°C/360°F/gas 4 and grease and line a 33 × 23 cm (13 × 9 inch) Swiss roll tin.

2. Sift together the flour, cocoa powder and baking powder.

3. Whisk together the egg yolks and sugar until stiff. Fold in the ground walnuts. In a separate bowl, whisk the egg whites until stiff. Fold the egg whites into the egg yolk, sugar and walnut mix, then fold in the hot water. Finally, fold in the dry ingredients. Pour onto the tin and spread evenly and bake on the middle shelf for 20 minutes.

4. Lay a piece of greaseproof parchment on top of a damp tea towel and sprinkle with caster sugar. When baked, turn the sponge out onto the parchment, remove the greaseproof parchment the cake was cooked in and immediately roll the sponge up. Leave on a wire tray until cold.

5. To make the filling, whisk the cream until firm. Unroll the sponge and spread most of the cream on top. Sprinkle the chopped walnuts over the cream.

6. Gently roll up the sponge and sprinkle the top with caster sugar. Decorate with the remaining cream, walnuts and pieces of chocolate.

~ Apple, Date & Coconut Cake ~

A wonderfully fruity cake.

Serves 8–10

285 g (10 oz) self-raising flour
60 g (2 oz) desiccated coconut
115 g (4 oz) dates, chopped
115 g (4 oz) butter
60 g (2 oz) vegetable fat
170 g (6 oz) caster sugar
1 medium-sized apple, peeled and cored
3 large eggs, beaten

1. Preheat the oven to 180°C/360°F/gas 4 and grease and fully line a 15 cm (6 inch) round cake tin.

2. Sift the flour into a bowl then stir in the coconut. Add the dates. Rub in the butter and vegetable fat until the mixture resembles fine breadcrumbs.

3. Stir in the sugar. Chop half of the apple into small squares and add to mixture. Beat the eggs and stir into the mixture, blending the ingredients evenly.

4. Spoon the mixture into the tin and slice the remaining apple and place on top. Bake on the middle shelf for 1¾ hours. After baking, leave to cool in the tin before removing.

⊸ *Hurrell Loaf* ⊸

This dense cake tastes best when buttered generously.

Serves 16

170 g (6 oz) wholemeal plain flour
115 g (4 oz) self-raising flour, sifted
½ tsp baking powder
a pinch of nutmeg
170 g (6 oz) sultanas
60 g (2 oz) walnuts, chopped
115 g (4 oz) demerara sugar
225 ml (7½ fl oz) black treacle
200 ml (7 fl oz) milk

1. Preheat the oven to 170°C/340°F/gas 3 and lightly grease and base line a 900 g (2 lb) loaf tin.

2. Place the wholemeal flour in a bowl, sift in the self-raising flour together with the baking powder and nutmeg. Stir in the sultanas, walnuts and sugar.

3. Pour the treacle into a saucepan, add the milk and stir over a low heat until the liquids combine. Pour the liquid into the dry ingredients and mix well.

4. Spoon the mixture into the tin and bake on the middle shelf for 1–1¼ hours. Leave for 15 minutes then turn out onto a wire tray.

❧ Crunchy Hazelnut Cake ❧

This nutty cake is easy to prepare. If you find flaked hazelnuts are difficult to come by, buy whole ones and chop them roughly with a sharp knife on a steady board.

Serves 16

For decoration:

60 g (2 oz) flaked hazelnuts

For the cake:

130 g (4½ oz) butter
215 g (7½ oz) caster sugar
3 large eggs
170 g (6 oz) ground hazelnuts
515 g (1 lb 2 oz) self-raising flour, sifted
¼ tsp salt
milk, as required

1. Preheat the oven to 190°C/370°F/gas 5 and grease a 23 cm (9 inch) ring tin.

2. Place the flaked hazelnuts evenly around the base of the tin. Cream the butter, then add the sugar and beat until light and fluffy.

3. Beat in the eggs, one at a time. Mix in the ground hazelnuts, then fold in the sifted flour and salt, with sufficient milk to make a fairly soft consistency.

4. Spoon the mixture into the tin and bake
on the middle shelf for 30 minutes at
190°C/370°F/gas 5, and for a further 30–45
minutes, or until baked, at 160°C/320°F/gas
2½. After baking, leave the cake in the tin for
30 minutes then turn out onto a wire tray to
cool.

~ *Strawberry and Almond* ~ Cake

A decadent, flavoursome cake that needs a little time set aside to prepare. Try substituting other soft fruits, such as fresh raspberries, peaches, nectarines and blackberries, for the strawberries.

Serves 16

For the cake:

3 large eggs
85 g (3 oz) caster sugar
85 g (3 oz) plain flour
30 g (1 oz) butter, melted
a couple of drops of almond essence

For the filling:

115 g (4 oz) butter
85 g (3 oz) caster sugar
85 g (3 oz) ground almonds
150 ml (¼ pint) thick cream
6 tbsp amaretto liqueur
225 g (8 oz) fresh strawberries

For the topping:

150 ml (¼ pint) thick cream
a handful of toasted flaked almonds

Mary's Tip

It is important to allow the cake time to cool on a wire tray. Trapped steam will be retained in the cake if it is left in its tin, which will make the cake heavy.

1. Preheat the oven to 180°C/360°F/gas 4 and grease and fully line a 900 g (2 lb) loaf tin.

2. For the cake, whisk the eggs and sugar together in a bowl sitting on a pan of hot water, until the mixture is light and thick and holds the shape of a figure of 8. Sieve the flour and lightly fold into the mixture. Blend in the melted butter and the almond essence with the last of the flour.

3. Immediately pour into the tin and bake on the middle shelf for 25 minutes. After baking, turn out onto a wire tray until cold. Then slice into three layers.

4. For the filling, beat together the butter and the sugar until light and fluffy. Beat in the ground almonds. Beat in the cream a little at a time to avoid curdling, then beat in the liqueur.

5. Re-line the tin with the greaseproof parchment, then grease the parchment lightly with butter. Place the bottom layer of sponge into the tin and sprinkle with liqueur, then place in the strawberries cut in half. Cover with half the filling, then repeat step 7 with the middle layer of the sponge. Place the last slice of sponge on top, sprinkle with liqueur and chill overnight.

6. Turn out onto the serving plate. Decorate with whipped cream, strawberries and flaked almonds.

TEATIME TREATS

~ojo~

The cakes in this section are, generally speaking, quick and easy to make, and they taste great, too.

~ojo~ Cupcakes ~ojo~

Quick to make, these delicious and beautifully presented cupcakes are sure to wow. Most online cake suppliers sell sugar flower decorations, and feel free to experiment with different styles of decoration.

Makes 12

For the cake:

115g (4oz) butter
145g (5oz) self-raising flour
145g (5oz) caster sugar
3 tbsp milk
2 eggs
½ teaspoon vanilla extract

For decoration:

buttercream (see page 41)
sugar flowers

1. Pre-heat the oven to 180°C/360°F/gas 4 and place 12 muffin cases into a muffin tin.

2. Place the cake ingredients into a large bowl and blend until smooth.

3. Spoon the mixture into the muffin cases and bake on the middle shelf for approximately 20–25 minutes.

4. Remove from the oven and take the cases out of the tin and cool on a wire rack completely.

5. Make the buttercream and spoon or pipe onto the top of the cooled cakes. Decorate with sugar flowers.

Mary's Tip

If you choose to pipe your buttercream onto the cakes, place the buttercream in the fridge for a few minutes before using to stop it from melting.

❦ *Golden Syrup Cake* ❦

This cake freezes well, but make sure you wait for it to defrost before sprinkling it with demerara sugar. It tastes best within 3 days of cooking or defrosting.

Serves 8–10

For the cake:

225 g (8 oz) butter
115 g (4 oz) demerara sugar
8 tbsp golden syrup
4 large eggs
225g (8 oz) self-raising flour, sifted

For the topping:

15g (½ oz) demerara sugar

1. Preheat the oven to 180°C/360°F/gas 4 and grease and base line a 15 cm (6 inch) round cake tin.

2. Cream the butter, sugar and syrup together until light and fluffy. Thoroughly beat in the egg, a little at a time. Sift and gently fold in the flour.

3. Spoon the mixture into the tin and bake on the middle shelf for 55 minutes. Leave in the tin for 10 minutes, then turn out onto a wire tray to cool. Sprinkle the top with demerara sugar.

‑ઓ‑ **Battenberg** ‑ઓ‑

This delicious cake tastes better home-made than any of the shop-bought varieties.

Serves 8–12

For the cake:

225 g (8 oz) butter
225 g (8 oz) caster sugar
4 large eggs, lightly beaten
225 g (8 oz) plain flour, sifted
1 tsp baking powder
pink food colouring
¼ tsp almond essence
½ tsp vanilla essence

For the filling:

seedless raspberry jam as required

For the covering:

225 g (8 oz) marzipan
caster sugar for rolling
200 g (7 oz) apricot jam

Mary's Tip

Go gently with the pink food colouring – the pink can be a very light shade to achieve the desired effect. Bakers often use a hard pink in the shops to attract the eye, but it is not necessary in the home-made variety.

1. Preheat the oven to 180°C/360°F/gas 4 and grease and base line two 900 g (2 lb) loaf tins.

2. Beat the butter and sugar together until light and fluffy. Then thoroughly beat in the egg, a little at a time. Sift the flour and baking powder together and blend into the batter using a spoon until the mixture is clear.

3. Divide the mixture in half by weight into separate bowls. Mix a few drops of pink food colouring and the almond essence into one batter, and the vanilla into the other. Place into separate tins and bake on the middle shelf for 40–45 minutes.

4. When baked turn out onto a wire tray to cool. Trim the sides then cut both cakes into six equal strips and layer with the jam filling.

5. Roll out the marzipan, using caster sugar as dusting. Warm the apricot jam, brush onto the marzipan and wrap around the cake. Crimp a pattern on the top.

❦ Banana Tea Bread ❦

This delicious cake tastes best if you use overripe bananas.

Serves 12

200 g (7 oz) self-raising flour
¼ tsp bicarbonate of soda
½ tsp salt
85 g (3 oz) butter
115 g (4 oz) caster sugar
2 large eggs
225 g (8 oz) bananas, mashed
2 tbsp golden syrup
225 g (8 oz) mixed dried fruit
115 g (4 oz) nuts, roughly chopped

Mary's Tip
Wrap the cake in foil and keep for a day before serving sliced and buttered.

1. Preheat the oven to 180°C/360°F/gas 4 and lightly grease and base line a 900 g (2 lb) loaf tin.

2. Sift together the flour, bicarbonate of soda and salt into a bowl. Rub in the butter until the mixture resembles breadcrumbs.

3. Beat the eggs, mashed bananas and syrup together and then stir into the mixture.

4. Stir in the dried fruit and nuts, then place the mixture into the tin and bake on the middle shelf for 1¼ hours. Turn out onto a wire tray to cool.

~ Apple and Walnut ~ Tea Bread

A delicious and moist tea bread.

Serves 8–10

225 g (8 oz) self-raising flour
a pinch of salt
1 tsp mixed spice
115 g (4 oz) butter
115 g (4 oz) caster sugar
2 large eggs
1 tbsp golden syrup
115 g (4 oz) sultanas
60 g (2oz) walnuts, chopped
1 medium cooking apple, peeled, cored and chopped
demerara sugar for sprinkling

1. Preheat the oven to 180°C/360°F/gas 4 and grease and line a 900 g (2 lb) loaf tin.

2. Sift together the flour, salt and mixed spice. Add the remaining ingredients.

3. Beat well using a spoon, then place the mixture into the tin and level. Sprinkle the top with a good layer of demerara sugar. Bake for 1 hour at 180°C/360°F/gas 4, then reduce the heat to 170°C/340°F/gas 3 and bake for 20 minutes. After baking, leave in the tin for 10 minutes then turn out to cool.

❧ *Apple and Sultana Scone* ❧

A delicious alternative to the traditional scone, these wedges taste great served still warm and spread with a little butter.

Serves 8

225 g (8 oz) self-raising flour, sifted
½ tsp salt
1 tsp baking powder
60 g (2 oz) butter
60 g (2 oz) caster sugar
1 medium-sized cooking apple, peeled, cored and diced
60 g (2 oz) sultanas
1 large egg, beaten
milk, as required
caster sugar for sprinkling

1. Preheat the oven to 200°C/400°F/gas 6 and lightly grease a 20 cm (8 inch) round sandwich or flan tin.

2. Sift together flour, salt and baking powder. Rub in the butter until the mixture resembles breadcrumbs, then add the sugar, apple and sultanas. Mix to a soft but not sticky dough with the beaten egg and a little milk.

3. Roll out into the shape of a circle on a floured surface to 0.5 cm (¼ inch) thickness and approximately 20 cm (8 inches) in diameter. Cut into 8 wedges and brush with a little milk and sugar before baking for approximately 20 minutes. Turn out onto a wire tray to cool.

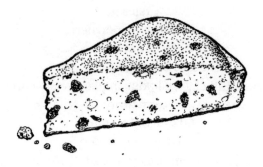

☙ *Caramel Sandwich Cake* ❧

Caramel is easy to make and tastes sensational, especially stirred into this delicious cake.

Serves 8

115 g (4 oz) butter
115 g (4 oz) granulated sugar
2 large eggs, separated
60 g (2 oz) cubed sugar
150 ml (¼ pint) hot milk
170 g (6 oz) plain flour, sifted
½ tsp baking powder
apricot jam, as required
icing sugar for dusting

Mary's Tip
When making caramel, allow the sugar to dissolve slowly over a gentle heat, without stirring, until it has turned brown.

1. Preheat the oven to 190°C/375°F/gas 5 and grease and flour two 18 cm (7 inch) round sandwich tins.

2. Cream together the butter and the sugar until light and fluffy, then beat in the egg yolks.

3. Make the caramel by heating the cubed sugar in a small pan until it melts and turns light brown. Cool slightly, then carefully add the hot milk and stir until the caramel is dissolved. When the caramel mixture is lukewarm, add it gradually to the creamed ingredients and beat together.

4. Sieve the flour and baking powder and add to the creamed ingredients, stirring well and adding a little more milk if necessary. The mixture should be of a soft, dropping consistency.

5. Stiffly beat the egg whites and fold them in. Pour the mixture into the tins and bake for approximately 30 minutes. Turn out onto a wire tray to cool, then fill with apricot jam and sprinkle the top with icing sugar.

～ Saffron Cake ～

This is a variation on the traditional Cornish saffron bread, which, like this version, is rich and golden-yellow in colour.

Serves 10–12

150 ml (¼ pint) water
a pinch of saffron strands
150 ml (¼ pint) milk
15 g (½ oz) dried yeast
a pinch of sugar
450 g (1 lb) strong plain flour
1 tsp salt
115 g (4 oz) butter
170 g (6 oz) currants
grated rind of ½ a lemon
30 g (1 oz) caster sugar

Mary's Tip
Do not open the oven door while the cake is cooking.

1. Boil the water and pour into a bowl with the saffron and leave to soak overnight.

2. Preheat the oven to 200°C/390°F/gas 6 and grease and base line two 900 g (2 lb) loaf tins.

3. Warm the milk and pour into a bowl with the yeast and a pinch of sugar. Leave in a warm place for 15 minutes until frothy.

4. Sift the flour and salt together. Rub in the butter until the mixture resembles breadcrumbs, then add the currants, lemon rind and sugar.

5. Strain the saffron liquid into a saucepan and discard the strands. Warm slightly then mix into the dry ingredients. Add the milk and yeast mixture and beat well to form a dough. Divide the mixture between the two tins, cover with a cloth and leave in a warm place for 1 hour.

6. Once the mixture has risen to two thirds the height of the tin, bake on the middle shelf for 15 minutes at 200°C/390°F/gas 6 then for a further 15–20 minutes at 180°C/360°F/gas 4. When baked, remove from the tin and leave to cool on a wire tray.

❧ Coffee and Sultana Cake ❧

This cake is packed full of flavour and interesting textures and is the perfect teatime treat.

Serves 16–20

For the cake:

145 g (5 oz) butter
145 g (5 oz) light brown soft sugar
2 large eggs
1½ tbsp coffee extract
225 g (8 oz) plain flour
½ tsp baking powder
115 g (4 oz) sultanas
milk as required

For the topping:

a handful of mixed chopped nuts
a handful of pecan nuts

1. Preheat the oven to 190°C/370°F/gas 5 and grease and base line a 900 g (2 lb) loaf tin.

2. Cream the butter and sugar and thoroughly beat in the eggs a little at a time. Beat in the coffee extract.

3. Sift together the flour and baking powder then stir into the mixture with the sultanas and sufficient milk to make a soft consistency.

4. Pour the mixture into the tin, sprinkle with chopped nuts and pecan nuts and bake on the middle shelf for 1–1¼ hours. After baking, leave for 10 minutes then turn out onto a wire tray to cool.

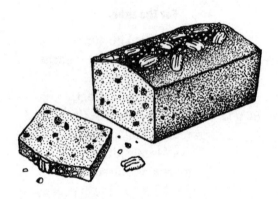

~ Apricot Nut Bread ~

Another nut-based tea bread, but this time paired with sweet, succulent dried apricots.

Serves 12–16

For the cake:

340 g (12 oz) self-raising flour
a pinch of salt
115 g (4 oz) caster sugar
145 g (5 oz) dried apricots, chopped
60 g (2 oz) blanched almonds, chopped
grated rind of 1 lemon
4 large eggs
150 ml (¼ pint) sour cream
60 g (2 oz) melted butter
milk, as required

For the topping:

115 g (4 oz) icing sugar
juice of 1 lemon

For decoration:

a few apricots, chopped

1. Preheat the oven to 170°C/340°F/gas 3 and grease and base line a 900 g (2 lb) loaf tin.

2. To make the cake, sift together the flour and salt into a bowl. Stir in the sugar, apricots, almonds and lemon rind, then make a well in the centre.

3. In a separate bowl, whisk together the eggs, cream and melted butter then stir into the mixture to make a soft, dropping consistency, adding a little milk if necessary.

4. Place the mixture into the tin and bake on the middle shelf for approximately 1½ hours. After baking, leave for 10 minutes then turn out onto a wire tray to cool.

5. To make the topping, sift the icing sugar into a bowl and beat in sufficient lemon juice to make a thickish soft icing. Pour onto the top of the cake then finish with a sprinkling of chopped apricots.

❧ Rich Jamaican Loaf ❧

A classic loaf cake that is simple and quick to make.

Serves 10

For the cake:

85 g (3 oz) butter
115 g (4 oz) light brown sugar
1 tbsp golden syrup
1 tbsp black treacle
2 large eggs, beaten
225 g (8 oz) bananas, mashed
225 g (8 oz) self-raising flour
1 tsp mixed spice
¼ tsp bicarbonate of soda
¼ tsp salt
225 g (8 oz) raisins

For the glaze:

2 tbsp golden syrup, warmed

1. Preheat the oven to 180°C/350°F/gas 4 and grease and line a 900 g (2 lb) loaf tin.

2. Cream the butter and sugar together until light and fluffy, then stir in the treacle and golden syrup. Add the eggs and banana, and mix well.

3. Sieve the flour, mixed spice, bicarbonate
of soda and salt, and add to the creamed
mixture with the raisins. Pour into the tin
and bake for approximately 1½ hours,
or until well risen and firm to the touch.
Remove from the tin and glaze the top with
the melted golden syrup.

~ Austrian Coffee Cake ~

Make sure you leave yourself plenty of time to make this cake.

Serves 16–20

For the cake:

250 g (9 oz) butter
225 g (8 oz) caster sugar
4 large eggs, separated
1 tsp grated lemon rind
285 g (10 oz) plain flour, sifted
1 tsp baking powder
30 g (1 oz) vanilla sugar
250 ml (9 fl oz) strong black coffee, cold
soft light brown sugar, as required
brandy, as required

For the coating:

600 ml (1 pt) whipping cream
coffee flavouring
85 g (3 oz) toasted flaked almonds
coffee powder for dusting

Mary's Tip
You can make your own vanilla sugar. Simply place a vanilla pod in a sealed container of sugar and leave until required.

1. Preheat the oven to 180°C/360°F/gas 4 and grease and fully line a 21.5 cm (8½ in) round cake tin.

2. Beat together the butter and caster sugar until light and fluffy. Thoroughly beat in the egg yolks, one at a time, then mix in the lemon rind.

3. Sift the flour and baking powder together. Whisk the egg whites with the vanilla sugar until stiff, then fold lightly into the creamed butter. Alternate mixing in spoonfuls of the egg white and flour until well blended. Pour into the tin and bake on the middle shelf for 1¼ hours. When baked, leave in the tin for 10 minutes, and then turn out onto a wire tray to cool.

4. Mix the coffee with a little sugar and brandy to taste. Place the cake back in the tin, prick the top with a skewer and brush on the liquid. Leave to soak for 2 hours.

5. For the coating, whip the cream and add a few drops of coffee flavouring. Remove the cake from the tin and coat the top and side with the cream. Sprinkle toasted flaked almonds onto the cake top and side followed by a dusting of cocoa powder. Chill and serve.

CELEBRATION CAKES

Though short, this section offers two failsafe recipes for two different festive occasions.

~ Simnel Cake ~

This popular Easter cake is perfect to serve to family and guests during the holidays.

Serves 16

For the cake:

170 g (6 oz) light brown soft sugar
170 g (6 oz) butter
3 large eggs
225 g (8 oz) plain wholemeal flour
170 g (6 oz) sultanas
115 g (4 oz) currants
60 g (2 oz) peel
60 g (2 oz) glacé cherries
½ tsp mixed spice
¼ tsp cinnamon
60 g (2 oz) ground almonds
grated rind of 1 lemon
grated rind of 1 small orange
milk, as required
115 g (4 oz) almond paste or marzipan

For decoration:

apricot jam, boiled
340 g (12 oz) almond paste or marzipan
1 egg, beaten

1. Preheat the oven to 160°C/320°F/gas 2½
and grease and line a 16.5 cm (6 inch) round
cake tin.

2. Cream the butter and sugar together until
light and fluffy. Thoroughly beat in the eggs,
one at a time.

3. Mix the remaining dry ingredients together,
then fold into the creamed butter, adding
milk to make the mixture soft. Spoon half the
mixture into the tin.

4. Roll out a 15 cm (6 inch) round of almond
paste and place on top of the first batch of
cake mixture. Cover with the remaining cake
mixture. Slightly hollow the top, then bake on
the middle shelf for 1 hour at 160°C/320°F/
gas 2½. Reduce the temperature to
150°C/300°F/gas 2 and continue baking for
a further 2–2½ hours. After baking, leave in
the tin for 30 minutes.

5. Remove the baking parchment and place the
cake onto a wire tray until cold. Brush the top
with boiling apricot jam. Divide the almond
paste for the top of the cake in half. Roll out
a 15 cm (6 inch) round with one half and

11 small balls with the other half. Place the circle of almond paste on top of the jam glaze and the balls round the edge of the cake.

6. Brush the marzipan with beaten egg and place the cake under a grill to colour.

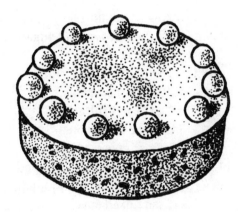

~ Glazed Nut Christmas Cake ~

Something to spice up the festivities.

Serves 30–36

For the cake:

225 g (8 oz) butter
225 g (8 oz) dark brown soft sugar
5 large eggs
285 g (10 oz) plain flour, sifted
450 g (1 lb) currants
340 g (12 oz) sultanas
340 g (12 oz) raisins
115 g (4 oz) mixed cut peel
115 g (4 oz) glacé cherries, chopped
60 g (2 oz) split almonds, chopped
½ tsp mixed spice
½ tsp nutmeg
½ tsp cinnamon
¼ tsp ginger
¼ tsp cloves
grated rind of ½ a lemon
grated rind of ¼ an orange
4 tbsp beer or barley wine

For the topping:

selection of nuts and cherries
egg whites, as required

Mary's Tip
Before you begin, tie a piece of thick brown paper round the outside of the cake tin to protect the sides.

1. Preheat the oven to 160°C/320°F/gas 2½ and grease and fully line a 20 cm (8 inch) square cake tin.

2. Cream the butter and sugar together, then slowly beat in the eggs. In a separate bowl, sift the flour and then mix in the remaining ingredients except the beer.

3. Stir the dry ingredients into the creamed mixture then add the beer or wine to form a wet consistency. Spoon the mixture into the tin and level.

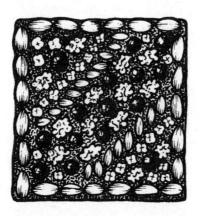

4. Create a decorative pattern on top of the uncooked cake using the nuts and cherries, then brush with egg white and bake for 30 minutes at 160°C/320°F/gas 2½. Then reduce the heat to 150°C/300°F/gas 2 and continue baking for a further 2½ hours. Finally, reduce the heat to 140°C/285°F/gas 1 and continue baking for 1 hour. In order to prevent the top of the cake from burning, cover the top with greaseproof parchment after 2½ hours cooking time.

COOKIES

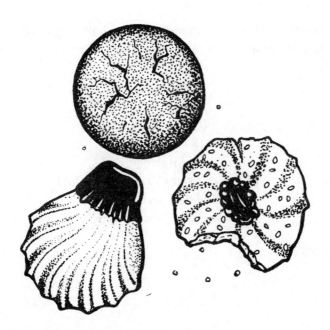

COOKIES, BISCUITS AND SHORTBREAD

~ele~

Quick to make and offering plentiful supplies, a batch of home-made biscuits tastes far superior to the shop-bought versions and cost a lot less, too.

~ele~ *Melting Moments* ~ele~

You'll find these delicious, buttery, melt in the mouth biscuits won't be in the tin for long.

Makes 16

60 g (2 oz) butter
60 g (2 oz) caster sugar
1 large egg
115 g (4 oz) self-raising flour, sifted
rolled oats, as required
a handful of glacé cherries

Mary's Tip
Allow the eggs to stand out of the refrigerator overnight to reach room temperature before using.

1. Preheat the oven to 180°C/360°F/gas 4 and grease two or three baking trays, depending on their size.

2. Cream the butter and sugar until light and fluffy, then gradually beat in the egg.

3. Gently fold in the sifted flour, then roll the mixture onto a floured surface and divide into 16 pieces.

4. Mould each piece into a ball then roll in the oats to cover. Place well apart onto the trays, flatten slightly then bake on the middle shelf for 15–20 minutes or until golden brown. After baking place half a cherry on each biscuit and leave until cold.

‐ঞ‐ **Bourbon** ‐ঞ‐

A classic biscuit that tastes wonderful dunked in a cup of tea or coffee.

Makes 18

For the biscuit:

115 g (4 oz) butter
85 g (3 oz) caster sugar
60 g (2 oz) golden syrup
1 tbsp egg, beaten
170 g (6 oz) plain flour
60 g (2 oz) semolina
30 g (1 oz) cocoa powder

For the topping:

30 g (1 oz) granulated sugar

For the filling:

115 g (4 oz) butter
170 g (6 oz) icing sugar, sifted
60 g (2 oz) plain or milk chocolate

1. Preheat the oven to 180°C/360°F/gas 4 and grease two or three baking trays, depending on their size.

2. For the biscuit, cream the butter, sugar and syrup together, then beat in the egg a little at a time. Sift together the flour, semolina and

cocoa powder, twice. Gradually fold into the creamed mixture.

3. Knead the mixture to form a smooth, well-blended dough. Do not over mix. Place the dough onto a lightly floured surface and gently roll it out into a square shape.

4. Using a ruler, cut into even-sized fingers. Prick each one with a fork then sprinkle on the granulated sugar. Place slightly apart on the trays and bake on the middle shelf for 15 minutes.

5. For the filling, beat the butter until light then beat in the icing sugar. Quickly beat in the melted chocolate. Sandwich the biscuits together with the filling.

Mary's Tip

To make the buttercream filing, use butter at room temperature.

❦ *Mincemeat Shortbread* ❦

This delicious shortbread is an excellent way of using up leftover mincemeat from Christmas.

Makes 8

115 g (4 oz) butter
60 g (2 oz) caster sugar
170 g (6 oz) plain flour, sifted
4 tbsp mincemeat
caster sugar for dusting

1. Preheat the oven to 170°C/340°F/gas 3 and grease a 21.5 cm (8½ inch) round sponge tin.

2. Cream the butter and sugar together then gradually work in the sifted flour and mincemeat. Knead the mixture until well blended.

3. Roll out onto a lightly floured surface then press evenly into the tin. Mark around the edge with a fork and press with the back of a spoon all around the inner edge. Cut into 8 sections then prick all over with a fork and bake for 25–30 minutes, or until golden brown. After baking cut again, sprinkle with caster sugar then leave until cold.

‑ఴ Almond Shortbread ఴ‑

Delicious and very quick to make, these biscuits will brighten up any teatime.

Makes 24

115 g (4 oz) butter
60 g (2 oz) caster sugar
115 g (4 oz) plain flour, sifted
60 g (2 oz) ground rice
30 g (1 oz) nibbed or chopped almonds
a handful of flaked almonds
caster sugar for dusting

1. Preheat the oven to 190°C/375°F/Gas 5. Lightly grease two or three baking trays, depending on their size.

2. Beat the butter until light and fluffy. Beat in the sugar thoroughly.

3. Lightly fold in the flour, ground rice and almonds. Gently roll out the mixture on to a lightly floured surface to a thickness of approximately 5 mm (¼ inch).

4. Cut into 5 cm (2 inch) circles and place on the baking trays. Press a flaked almond on the top of each and bake for 10–15 minutes or until light brown. Sprinkle with caster sugar, lift onto a wire rack and leave to cool.

~ Finnish Gingers ~

Try to make these biscuits as thin as possible for a crisp finished biscuit.

Makes 50

85 g (3 oz) butter
60 g (2 oz) caster sugar
115 g (4 oz) golden syrup
200 g (7 oz) self-raising flour, sifted
½ tsp ground cinnamon
½ tsp ground ginger
½ tsp ground cloves
½ tsp bicarbonate of soda
1 tsp water

1. Preheat the oven to 150°C/300°F/gas 2 and lightly grease two baking trays.

2. Melt the butter, sugar and syrup over a gentle heat. Sift the flour and spices into a separate bowl then stir into the mixture.

3. Dissolve the bicarbonate of soda in the water and mix in to form a soft dough. Cover the bowl and leave overnight in a cool place.

4. Mould the dough into a small loaf shape approximately 20 cm (8 inches) long. Cut into thin slices, place onto trays and bake on the middle shelf for 10–15 minutes or until golden brown.

⁓ Viennese Shells ⁓

These short biscuits are quick to make and look pretty as a picture when piped as shells, rosettes, fingers or stars. It's nice to vary the decoration – this recipe suggests using a mixture of glacé cherries and melted chocolate to adorn the finished biscuits.

Makes 30

For the biscuit:

170 g (6 oz) butter
60 g (2 oz) icing sugar, sifted
170 g (6 oz) plain flour

For decoration:

glacé cherries, halved
plain or milk chocolate, melted

1. Preheat the oven to 150°C/300°F/gas 2 and grease two or three baking trays, depending on their size.

2. Using a wooden spoon, beat the butter and icing sugar together until creamy. Gradually work in the flour to form a soft dough.

3. Place the mixture inside a piping bag fixed with a star-shaped nozzle, then pipe shell-shaped biscuits onto the trays. Place a half glacé cherry at the base of one third of the shells then bake the whole batch on the

middle shelf for 20–30 minutes or until lightly brown. Turn out onto a wire tray to cool.

4. When cold, dip half of the shells without glacé cherries into melted chocolate (see page 28), chill to set the chocolate and then serve.

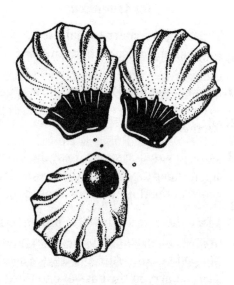

⬦ **Parkin** ⬦

A biscuit version of the parkin cake that originated in the north of England. This recipe uses golden syrup instead of the black treacle normally used to make the cake.

Makes 24

170 g (6 oz) plain flour
2 tsp ground ginger
1 tsp ground cinnamon
170 g (6 oz) oatmeal
60 g (2 oz) butter
60 g (2 oz) light brown soft sugar
225 g (8 oz) golden syrup
½ tsp bicarbonate of soda
2 tbsp milk

1. Preheat the oven to 170°C/340°F/gas 3 and grease two or three baking trays, depending on their size.

2. Sift the flour and spices together then mix in the oatmeal. Rub in the butter until the mixture resembles breadcrumbs. Stir in the sugar and the golden syrup.

3. Dissolve the bicarbonate of soda in 1 tbsp of milk and add to the rest of the mixture. Mix to form a soft dough, using the remaining milk if required. Divide the mixture in half and roll to a sausage shape.

4. Cut each roll into 12 pieces. Roll each piece into a ball between floured hands. Place onto the trays, position a split almond on top of each biscuit then bake on the middle shelf for 20 minutes or until golden brown. After baking leave the biscuits for 5 minutes then transfer them onto a wire rack to cool.

❧ Coffee Drops ☙

These thin and crispy biscuits spread themselves widely during the cooking process. They also tend to brown quickly, so keep a watchful eye on them.

Makes 36

60 g (2 oz) butter
60 g (2 oz) light brown soft sugar
85 g (3 oz) golden syrup
1 tbsp egg, beaten
2 tsp coffee essence
85 g (3 oz) self-raising flour
½ tsp ground cinnamon
a handful of chopped walnuts to decorate

1. Preheat the oven to 180°/360°F/gas 4 and grease your baking trays.

2. Cream the butter, sugar and syrup together. Beat in the egg then the coffee essence.

3. Sift the flour and cinnamon together then gradually blend into the mixture to form a soft, smooth dough.

4. Fill a piping bag with the mixture and pipe small bulbs spaced well apart onto the trays. Top with walnut pieces and bake on the middle shelf for approximately 15 minutes. Leave on the tray for 5 minutes before transferring to a wire tray to cool.

❧ *Gingerbread Snaps* ❧

This recipe suggests adding a variety of toppings to these rich, dark-coloured biscuits. But while these different finishes work well with each other, don't feel you have to try them all.

Makes 20

For the biscuits:

6 tbsp black treacle
85 g (3 oz) butter
60 g (2 oz) light brown soft sugar
225 g (8 oz) plain flour
½ tsp ground ginger
½ tsp ground coriander
¼ tsp bicarbonate of soda

or the toppings:

a selection of desiccated coconut, demerara sugar, oatmeal, flaked almonds and ginger pieces

1. Preheat the oven to 180°C/350°F/gas 4 and grease your baking trays.

2. Put the treacle, butter and sugar into a small saucepan and stir over a low heat until the butter has melted. Sift the remaining ingredients together into a bowl.

3. When the treacle has cooled mix it into the dry ingredients to form a soft, smooth dough. Turn out and divide in half. Roll both halves so they each form a 25 cm (10 inch) long sausage and cut both into 10 separate pieces.

4. Roll into balls and into any of the suggested toppings. Place onto trays and bake just above the middle shelf for 8–10 minutes.

Mary's Tip
When melting the treacle, butter and sugar ensure that the heat is low – the mixture should melt, not cook.

∽ Florentines ∽

Sweet, chewy and sticky, these treats make for excellent Christmas gifts.

Makes 20

85 g (3 oz) plain flour, sifted
60 g (2 oz) sultanas
115 g (4 oz) glacé cherries, chopped
170 g (6 oz) flaked almonds
170 g (6 oz) golden syrup
170 g (6 oz) butter
225 g (8 oz) plain or milk chocolate, to decorate

1. Preheat the oven to 190°C/375°F/gas 5 and prepare a baking tray with appropriate sized baking cases.

2. Mix together the flour, sultanas, glacé cherries and flaked almonds in a bowl. Place the syrup and butter into a saucepan and melt.

3. As soon as the butter has melted remove from the heat and stir in the mixed ingredients until well blended.

4. Spread small amounts into the baking cases or directly onto trays and bake on the middle shelf for 10–12 minutes. Leave to cool on the trays then coat the undersides with melted chocolate.

∼ Peanut Crisps ∼

The saltiness of peanut butter works beautifully with the sweetness of golden syrup in these delicious cookies.

Makes 20

60 g (2 oz) butter
60 g (2 oz) light brown soft sugar
60 g (2 oz) golden syrup
115 g (4 oz) crunchy peanut butter
85 g (3 oz) plain flour, sifted
30 g (1 oz) medium oatmeal
¼ tsp bicarbonate of soda
1 tbsp hot water
a little medium oatmeal to decorate

Mary's Tip
It is essential to measure bicarbonate of soda accurately to ensure perfect results.

1. Preheat the oven to 180°C/360°F/gas 4 and grease your baking trays.

2. Beat the butter, sugar, syrup and peanut butter together thoroughly, then work in the sifted flour and oatmeal. Dissolve the bicarbonate of soda in the hot water and stir into the mixture to form a soft dough.

3. Mould the mixture into a long roll, cut into 20 pieces then shape into rounds. Space apart on the baking trays, flatten and sprinkle with a little oatmeal, then bake on the middle shelf for 15 minutes or until golden brown. Leave for a few minutes then turn out onto a wire tray to cool.

❧ *Peanut Chews* ❧

Experiment with different flavours – finely chopped walnuts, will produce a stronger flavour than peanuts.

Makes 36

115 g (4 oz) butter
85 g (3 oz) low-fat cream cheese
½ tsp vanilla essence
170 g (6 oz) caster sugar
225 g (8 oz) plain flour, sifted
a pinch of salt
115 g (4 oz) peanuts, finely chopped

1. Preheat the oven to 190°C/375°F/gas 5 and grease your baking trays.

2. Blend the butter, cream cheese and vanilla essence together, then gradually beat in the sugar until light and creamy.

3. Sift the flour and salt together into the mixture, add the chopped peanuts and blend to a soft dough.

4. Mould the dough into a roll and cut into 36 pieces. Shape each cookie into rounds, place onto the trays and flatten slightly before marking with the back of a fork. Bake on the middle shelf for approximately 12 minutes or until golden brown around the edges. After baking leave on a wire tray to cool.

~ *Almond Macaroons* ~

For a little variety, omit the almonds from this recipe and dip half of the biscuits into melted chocolate when cool.

Makes 16

For the cookies:

170 g (6 oz) caster sugar
115 g (4 oz) ground almonds
1 tsp rice flour
1–2 egg whites

For decoration:

caster sugar for sprinkling
a handful of split almonds

1. Preheat the oven to 180°C/360°F/gas 4 and grease your baking trays.

2. Mix the sugar, ground almonds and rice flour together. In a separate bowl lightly whisk the egg whites.

3. Add sufficient beaten egg whites to the dry ingredients to form a stiff dough. Mould the dough into a long roll and cut into 16 pieces, then shape each piece into a ball.

4. Place onto the trays, allowing plenty of
room for spreading during baking. Brush
with the remaining egg white, place a split
almond on top of each, then sprinkle with a
little caster sugar. Bake on the middle shelf
for approximately 15 minutes or until light
brown.

~ə~ *Lemon Cookies* ~ə~

These little treats are a refreshing accompaniment to a nice cup of tea.

Makes 24

For the cookies:

85 g (3 oz) butter
60 g (2 oz) caster sugar
60 g (2 oz) golden syrup
grated rind of 1 lemon
1 egg yolk
115 g (4 oz) plain flour, sifted
30 g (1 oz) cornflour, sifted

For decoration:

icing sugar for dusting
lemon curd, as required

1. Preheat the oven to 170°C/340°F/gas 3 and grease your baking trays.

2. Cream the butter, sugar, syrup and lemon rind together well with a wooden spoon, then thoroughly beat in the egg yolk.

3. Sift the plain flour and cornflour together. Using a spatula, gradually fold the flours into the mixture to form a well blended dough. Mould the dough into a roll and cut into 24 pieces.

4. Roll each piece into a ball, place onto the trays and bake on the middle shelf for 15 minutes. Remove from the oven and press each top with the handle of a wooden spoon to form a well. Continue baking for another 5 minutes or until golden brown. When cold, dust with icing sugar then fill the tops with a small spoonful of lemon curd.

❦ Cornish Fairings ❦

Quick to prepare, and even quicker to cook, these traditional ginger biscuits will go down a treat.

Makes 24

225 g (8 oz) plain flour
¼ tsp salt
2 tsp baking powder
2 tsp bicarbonate of soda
2 tsp ground mixed spice
3 tsp ground ginger
1 tsp cinnamon
115 g (4 oz) butter
115 g (4 oz) caster sugar
170 g (6 oz) golden syrup

Mary's Tip
Careful baking is essential to avoid over colouring, especially when using a fan oven.

1. Preheat the oven to 180°F/360°F/gas 4 and grease your baking trays.

2. Sift together the flour, salt, baking powder, bicarbonate of soda, mixed spice, ginger and cinnamon into a bowl. Rub in the butter until the mixture resembles breadcrumbs, then stir in the sugar. Pour in the syrup and blend together to form a soft, smooth dough.

3. Roll the dough into walnut-sized pieces, place onto the trays and bake for 7 minutes or until golden brown. Be careful not to move the trays during baking as it may cause the biscuits to collapse.

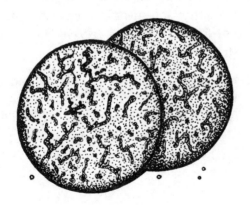

~ Chocolate Crunchies ~

These cookies are quite hard and crunchy and are best kept in an airtight container to keep them crisp.

Makes 24

170 g (6 oz) plain flour, sifted
a pinch of salt
85 g (3 oz) butter
115 g (4 oz) demerara sugar
1 large egg
85 g (3 oz) plain chocolate, cut into tiny pieces

1. Preheat the oven to 180°C/360°F/gas 4 and grease your baking trays.

2. Sift the flour and salt together twice. Cream the butter and sugar in a separate mixing bowl, then beat in the egg. Fold in the flour, then add the chocolate pieces.

3. Mould the mixture into a long roll and divide into 24 pieces. Place onto the trays and press with the back of a fork. Bake on the middle shelf for 10–15 minutes or until firm. Leave on the trays to cool.

~ Hazelnut Clusters ~

These oaty, nutty treats will pep up any lunchbox or biscuit tin.

Makes 30

115 g (4 oz) plain flour
225 g (8 oz) rolled oats
115 g (4 oz) hazelnuts, chopped
115 g (4 oz) light brown soft sugar
115 g (4 oz) butter
1 large egg, beaten
1 tbsp black treacle

1. Preheat the oven to 200°C/400°F/gas 5 and lightly grease your baking trays.

2. Sift the flour into a bowl then mix in the oats, hazelnuts and sugar.

3. Melt the butter in a saucepan, then stir into the dry ingredients together with the egg and the treacle. Mix until well blended.

4. Form into small rounds approximately 1 cm (½ inch) thick, place onto the trays and bake on the middle shelf for 15–20 minutes. Leave on the trays for 5 minutes before transferring to a wire tray to cool.

~⊛~ *Golden Oaties* ~⊛~

A light, sweet, buttery treat to perk up the most grey afternoon.

Makes 30

115 g (4 oz) butter
2 tbsp golden syrup
115 g (4 oz) self-raising flour
115 g (4 oz) light brown soft sugar
115 g (4 oz) rolled oats
1 tsp ground ginger
2 tsp warm water

1. Preheat the oven to 150°C/300°F/gas 2 and grease your baking trays.

2. Gently melt the butter with the syrup in a saucepan. Mix the flour, sugar, oats and ginger in a mixing bowl and stir in the melted butter together with the warm water until well blended.

3. Leave to cool for 5 minutes then mould into balls and place well apart on the trays. Bake on the middle shelf for approximately 25 minutes. After baking leave on the trays for 5 minutes before transferring to a wire tray to cool.

BARS AND SLICES

~ↄ⌣ↄ~

In this section you will find a host of recipes for cakes and bars that are easy to grab when you're on the go and feeling a little peckish.

~ↄ⌣ **Fruit and Nut Bars** ↄ⌣~

These little lunchbox fillers will power you through the afternoon, and beyond.

Makes 24

225 g (8 oz) hazelnuts, roughly chopped
225 g (8 oz) dates, roughly chopped
115 g (4 oz) glacé cherries, roughly chopped
1 tsp vanilla essence
2 large eggs
200 g (7 oz) soft light brown sugar
60 g (2 oz) plain flour
1 tsp baking powder
icing sugar for dusting

1. Preheat the oven to 180°C/360°F/gas 4 and grease an 18 × 28 cm (7 × 11 inch) shallow baking tin.

2. Mix the hazelnuts, dates and cherries together in a bowl with the vanilla essence. In a separate bowl whisk the eggs and sugar together until light and fluffy. Stir into the mixed fruit.

3. Sift the flour and baking powder together and fold into the mixture until well blended. Spread into the tin and bake on the middle shelf for approximately 40– 45 minutes. After baking, cut into bars while still warm.

Mary's Tip
These bars improve with keeping, but remember to store them in an airtight container.

⚬ *Jam Fingers* ⚬

This sweet version of a jam sandwich will have your taste buds tingling.

Makes 12

225 g (8 oz) plain flour, sifted
1 tsp baking powder
2 tsp ground cinnamon
115 g (4 oz) butter
85 g (3 oz) golden syrup
1 egg yolk
jam to fill
icing sugar for dusting

Mary's Tip
Rinse measures and spoons in hot water before use as any syrup can then be scraped off cleanly without waste.

1. Preheat the oven to 190°C/375°F/gas 5 and grease a 20 cm (8 inch) square, shallow baking tin.

2. Sift together the flour, baking powder and cinnamon, then rub in the butter until the mixture resembles breadcrumbs. Mix in the sugar and egg yolk to form a smooth dough.

3. Divide the dough in half. Roll out and fit one portion evenly into the tin and spread a generous amount of jam filling on top. Place the remaining portion of rolled-out dough on top of the jam. Bake on the middle shelf for 30 minutes. After baking, leave to cool before cutting into fingers.

✤ Chocolate Walnut Bars ✤

These indulgent bars make perfect mid-afternoon snacks. Why not try experimenting with different flavours by using black treacle as a substitute for golden syrup, and adding a sprinkling of desiccated coconut on top.

Makes 16

For the base:

85 g (3 oz) butter
115 g (4 oz) plain flour
85 g (3 oz) rolled oats
½ tsp baking powder
115 g (4 oz) demerara sugar

For the topping:

85 g (3 oz) plain chocolate
85 g (3 oz) milk chocolate
60 g (2 oz) butter
225 g (8 oz) golden syrup
60 g (2 oz) plain flour
1 tsp vanilla essence
115 g (4 oz) walnuts, chopped
60 g (2 oz) white chocolate to decorate

1. Preheat the oven to 180°C/360°F/gas 4 and grease an 18 × 28 cm (7 × 11 inch) shallow baking tin.

2. For the base, melt the butter, remove from the heat and stir in the flour, oats, baking powder and sugar. Mix well then spread evenly into the tin and bake for 10 minutes.

3. For the topping, melt the plain and milk chocolate with the butter and syrup. Remove from the heat and stir in the flour, vanilla essence and walnuts.

4. Spread on top of the cooked base and return to the oven for 20–25 minutes. Cool in the tin for 10 minutes, then loosen around the edges and cut into bars. Place a wire tray over the tin, upturn and remove the tin. Place a second wire tray on the top and upturn again. Leave to cool.

5. Melt the white chocolate and drizzle on the top in fine swirling lines. Separate the bars when the chocolate has set.

∘ɕᴏ- *Marbled Bars* -ɕᴏ∘

An attractive and very tasty marriage of plain and chocolate sponge, these marbled bars are perfect for feeding the family.

Makes 16

1 tbsp cocoa powder
1 tbsp boiling water
170 g (6 oz) butter
170 g (6 oz) caster sugar
170 g (6 oz) self-raising flour
1½ tsp baking powder
3 large eggs

1. Preheat the oven to 170°C/340°F/gas 3 and grease and fully line an 18 × 28 cm (7 × 11 inch) shallow baking tin.

2. Blend the cocoa powder and hot water together and leave to cool. Place the remaining ingredients into a mixing bowl and beat for 2–3 minutes on a medium speed.

3. Divide the mixture into two equal portions. Stir the cocoa mixture into one portion until well blended.

4. Using a dessertspoon, place alternate spoonfuls of the mixture into the tin and then bake on the middle shelf for approximately

25 minutes or when firm to the touch. Leave
to cool in the tin for 10 minutes then turn out
onto a wire tray to cool. Slice into portions
once cool.

Mary's Tip

When cooked this tray bake should spring back
when lightly pressed on the top, and have slightly
shrunk from the sides of the tin.

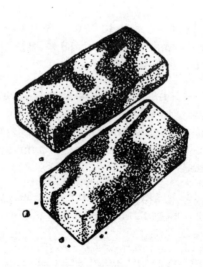

~ご~ *Orange Bars* ~ご~

If you're not keen on the taste of oranges, why not try using lemon or lime for the biscuit and the topping instead.

Makes 16

For the base:

170 g (6 oz) plain flour, sifted
60 g (2 oz) semolina
85 g (3 oz) caster sugar
170 g (6 oz) butter
finely grated rind of 1 orange

For the topping:

170 g (6 oz) icing sugar, sifted
orange juice, as required

1. Preheat the oven to 170°C/340°F/gas 3 and grease an 18 cm (7 inch) square, shallow baking tin.

2. Mix the flour, semolina and sugar together in a bowl. Rub in the butter until the mixture resembles breadcrumbs. Mix in the orange rind.

3. Spoon the mixture into the tin and firm down evenly with a spatula. Bake on the middle shelf for approximately 45 minutes or until firm to the touch.

4. For the topping, mix the icing sugar and orange juice to make a thick coating consistency. Spread over the biscuit when baked and return to the oven for a further 10 minutes. Leave in the tin to cool before cutting into bars.

Mary's Tip
Be careful not to overbake the topping, and make sure you scrub the orange thoroughly before grating to remove the wax coating.

❧ *Coconut Bars* ❧

These dense, sweet treats won't be around long enough to reach the biscuit tin.

Makes 24

For the base:

145 g (5 oz) plain flour
85 g (3 oz) butter
85 g (3 oz) caster sugar
2 tbsp cold water to mix (approx.)

For the filling:

2 large eggs
60 g (2 oz) light brown soft sugar
1 tsp vanilla essence
60 g (2 oz) plain flour
¼ tsp salt
1½ tsp baking powder
285 g (10 oz) desiccated coconut

For the topping:

30 g (1 oz) desiccated coconut
225 g (8 oz) icing sugar
30 g (1 oz) butter
2 tbsp lemon juice

1. Preheat the oven to 180°C/360°F/gas 4 and grease an 18 × 28 cm (7 × 11 inch) shallow baking tin.

2. To make the base, sift the flour into a bowl, add the butter and rub between fingers until the mixture resembles breadcrumbs. Mix in the sugar. Add the water and mix with a knife. Knead to form a pastry, then roll out and fit into the tin. Prick with a fork then bake for 20 minutes or until golden brown.

3. For the filling, whisk the eggs, sugar and vanilla essence together in a bowl until light and fluffy. Sift the flour, salt and baking powder together then fold into the mixture with the coconut to form a crumbly texture.

4. Spread onto the cooked base and lightly press evenly with a spatula. Bake in the oven for 10 minutes then leave in the tin until cold.

5. For the topping, toast the coconut until golden brown. Sift the icing sugar into a large bowl, melt the butter and stir into the icing sugar with the lemon juice.

6. Spread over the top using a serrated scraper or fork to create a wavy pattern. Sprinkle with the toasted coconut then cut into squares.

~ Chill Bars ~

A delicious snack!

Makes 28

For the base:

285 g (10 oz) golden syrup
225 g (8 oz) peanut butter
1 tsp vanilla essence
225 g (8 oz) cereal bran
60 g (2 oz) peanuts, chopped

For the topping:

115 g (4 oz) plain or milk chocolate

1. Grease an 18 × 28 cm (7 × 11 inch) shallow baking tin.

2. Mix the syrup and peanut butter together in a large saucepan and cook over a medium heat, stirring until the mixture begins to boil. Remove from the heat and stir in the vanilla essence, cereal bran and peanuts.

3. Spread the mixture into the prepared tin, pressing lightly and evenly. Chill for 1 hour, then turn out onto greaseproof parchment

4. Melt the chocolate (see page 28) and spread over the top using a palette knife or serrated scraper. Cut into squares when set.

TRAY BAKES AND FLAPJACKS

~⊙⊙~

The recipes in this section straddle the worlds of cakes and cookies.

~⊙⊙~ Lemon Fingers ~⊙⊙~

If you're not keen on lemons, you could try flavouring these cakes with oranges or limes instead.

Makes 30

For the cake:

145 g (5 oz) butter
145 g (5 oz) caster sugar
grated rind of 1 lemon
3 large eggs
145 g (5 oz) self-raising flour

For the topping:

200 g (7 oz) icing sugar, sifted
2 tbsp lemon juice
a little water
a few drops of yellow food colouring
sugar paste lemons or lemon slices to decorate

1. Preheat the oven to 180°C/360°F/gas 4 and grease and line a 18 × 28 cm (7 × 11 inch) shallow baking tin.

2. For the cake, place all the ingredients in a mixing bowl and beat for 3 minutes on a medium speed or for 5 minutes by hand with a wooden spoon.

3. Spread the mixture evenly into the prepared tin and bake on the middle shelf for 30–35 minutes. After baking, place on a wire tray, remove the greaseproof parchment and leave until cold.

4. To make the topping, mix the ingredients together to form a smooth, but not too soft, icing. Spread over the sponge and leave to set before cutting. Decorate as required.

～ Almond Crunch Fingers ～

Like a flapjack but with the added benefit of a pastry base topped with a touch of jam, these delicious slices are guaranteed to delight.

Makes 20

170 g (6 oz) plain flour, sifted
85 g (3 oz) butter
water to mix
apricot jam, as required
85 g (3 oz) golden syrup
85 g (3 oz) butter
30 g (1 oz) light brown soft sugar
115 g (4 oz) rolled oats
a few drops of almond essence

Mary's Tip
Flaked almonds can be added to the top of the mixture before baking.

1. Preheat the oven to 190°C/375°F/gas 5 and grease an 18 × 28 cm (7 × 11 inch) shallow baking tin.

2. Place the flour into a bowl and rub in the butter. Mix in sufficient water to make a smooth pastry. Line the tin and crimp the edge with a fork, then spread with jam.

3. Warm the syrup, butter and sugar together gently in a saucepan until the butter has melted. Stir in the oats and almond essence to taste.

4. Spoon the mixture over the jam and spread evenly with a spatula. Bake on the middle shelf for approximately 25 minutes or until golden brown. After baking leave to cool then cut into fingers.

~o⊘~ **Redberry Frangipan** ~o⊘~

A pastry base topped with aromatic frangipan, tart berries and an attractive pastry trellis makes this is an ideal dessert. It tastes delicious served warm with cream and sprinkled with demerara sugar.

Makes 12

For the base:

145 g (5 oz) plain flour, sifted
145 g (5 oz) self-raising flour, sifted
85 g (3 oz) caster sugar
145 g (5 oz) butter, cubed
1 large egg
1 tbsp milk

For the filling:

85 g (3 oz) caster sugar
115 g (4 oz) butter
2 large eggs
115 g (4 oz) ground almonds
60 g (2 oz) seedless raspberry jam
60 g (2 oz) frozen cranberries
60 g (2 oz) frozen raspberries
milk for glaze
caster sugar for sprinkling

1. Preheat the oven to 190°C/375°F/gas 5 and lightly grease a 30 × 10 cm (12 × 4 inch) fluted rectangular flan tin.

2. For the base, sift the flours together into a large bowl. Stir in the sugar then rub in the butter until the mixture resembles fine breadcrumbs. Make a well in the centre, add the egg and milk, stir then knead to a soft, smooth dough. Chill for 30 minutes then line the tin with the dough and prick with a fork, making sure you reserve some dough for the trellis on the top.

3. For the filling, cream the sugar and butter together until light and fluffy. Gradually beat in the eggs and ground almonds.

4. Spread the raspberry jam over the base using a palette knife. Spread the filling over the jam and then sprinkle the frozen cranberries and raspberries on top.

5. Roll out the remaining dough, cut into narrow strips, fix in a trellis pattern on top of the fruit and glaze with milk. Bake on the middle shelf at 190°C/375°F/gas 5 for 20 minutes, then reduce the heat to 180°C/360°F/gas 4 and continue baking for a further 25–30 minutes. Sprinkle with sugar and leave to cool in the tin. Cut when cold.

⊸◦⊸ *Apple and Date Shortcake* ⊸◦⊸

Sweet and delicious slices.

Makes 12–16

115 g (4 oz) butter
85 g (3 oz) caster sugar
1 large egg
170 g (6 oz) self-raising flour, sifted
225 g (8 oz) cooking apples, peeled, cored, chopped
and cooked
115 g (4 oz) dates, chopped
caster sugar for dusting

1. Preheat the oven to 180°C/360°F/gas 4
and lightly grease an 18 cm (7 inch) square
shallow tin.

2. Beat the butter and sugar together until light
and fluffy. Gradually beat in the egg a little at
a time.

3. Stir the sifted flour into the mixture to form a
well-blended pastry. Divide into two pieces,
roll out both and place one piece in the tin.

4. Mix the apples and dates together and spread
on top of the base layer of pastry. Place the
remaining piece of pastry on top and bake
on the middle shelf for 35–40 minutes. When
baked sprinkle with caster sugar and cut into
bars when cold.

~ Apple and Sultana ~ Tray Bake

An attractive looking and very tasty tray bake that is perfect eaten on its own or with a scoop of ice cream.

Makes 12

For the base:

255 g (9 oz) self-raising flour, sifted
a pinch of salt
2 tbsp cornflour
½ tsp ground cloves
85 g (3 oz) butter
1 tsp grated lemon rind
70 g (2½ oz) light brown soft sugar
1 egg yolk
6 tbsp milk

For the filling:

570 g (1¼ lb) cooking apples, peeled, cored
and sliced
1 tbsp lemon juice
2 tbsp water
1 tsp grated lemon rind
60 g (2 oz) sultanas
2 tbsp golden syrup
icing sugar for dusting

1. Preheat the oven to 220°C/425°F/gas 7 and lightly grease an 18 × 28 cm (7 × 11 inch) shallow baking tin.

2. To make the base, sift the flour, salt, cornflour and ground cloves into a bowl. Rub in the butter until the mixture resembles fine breadcrumbs. Stir in the lemon rind and sugar, then bind to a pliable dough with the egg yolk and milk. Knead on a lightly floured surface until smooth, then wrap in polythene and chill whilst making the filling.

3. To make the filling, place the apples, lemon juice and water in a pan and cook gently until just tender. Remove from the heat, stir in the lemon rind, fruit and syrup then leave until cold.

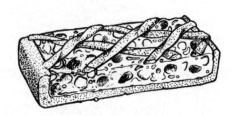

4. Roll out two thirds of the dough and line the tin. Spread the filling evenly over the pastry. Roll out the remaining dough and cut into narrow strips. Twist the strips, using a little dab of water to fix.

5. Bake on the middle shelf at 220°C/425°F/ gas 7 for 10 minutes, then reduce the heat to 190°C/375°F/gas 5 and bake for a further 20 minutes or until golden brown and the pastry is cooked through. After baking, dust with icing sugar then leave to cool in the tin before cutting into slices.

⊸ⱺ *Apricot Fruit Fingers* ⱺ⊸

The wholemeal flour and selection of fruits and nuts in this recipe should make you feel like you're eating something healthy, even though you're still treating yourself.

Makes 24

For the base:

115 g (4 oz) plain wholemeal flour
115 g (4 oz) plain flour, sifted
1 tsp ground cinnamon
170 g (6 oz) butter
2 tbsp golden syrup

For the topping:

60 g (2 oz) plain wholemeal flour
170 g (6 oz) no-soak apricots, roughly chopped
85 g (3 oz) mixed nuts, roughly chopped
60 g (3 oz) glacé cherries, roughly chopped
1 large egg, beaten
125 ml (4 fl oz) unsweetened orange juice

1. Preheat the oven to 190°C/375°F/gas 5 and grease an 18 × 28 cm (7 × 11 inch) shallow baking tin.

2. For the base, place the wholemeal flour, the sifted plain flour and cinnamon into a bowl. Mix in the butter and syrup. Stir well to form a soft dough then roll out and fit evenly into the tin and bake on the middle shelf for 20 minutes.

3. For the topping, mix together the wholemeal flour, chopped fruits and nuts until well blended. Stir in the egg and orange juice.

4. Spread the topping on the cooked base and bake for a further 15 minutes, or until the topping is set but still soft. Leave to cool in the tin then cut into bars.

~·☙ *Flapjacks* ❧·~

Quick to make and packed full of nutritious oats, these classic treats are the perfect energy-boosting snack for kids and adults on the go.

Makes 12

170 g (6 oz) rolled oats
115 g (4 oz) light brown soft sugar
85 g (3 oz) butter
60 g (2 oz) golden syrup

1. Preheat the oven to 180°/360°F/gas 4 and grease a 28 × 18 cm (11 × 7 inch) shallow baking tin.

2. Mix the oats and sugar together in a bowl. Melt the butter and syrup together in a saucepan.

3. Mix the dry ingredients into the saucepan until well blended then spoon into the greased tin. Press the mixture evenly into the tin and bake on the middle shelf for 20 minutes or until golden brown. After baking leave to cool slightly then cut into fingers or bars. Turn out when cold.

～⊙～ Brownies ～⊙～

This rich, moist tray bake will store very well if left uncut in an airtight tin. And, if you are watching the calories, you can always forgo the topping – the brownie tastes just as good.

Makes 24

For the brownie:

115 g (4 oz) butter
115 g (4 oz) plain chocolate
115 g (4 oz) dark brown soft sugar
115 g (4 oz) self-raising flour, sifted
a pinch of salt
2 large eggs
60 g (2 oz) walnuts, chopped
1–2 tbsp milk

For the topping:

115 g (4 oz) plain chocolate
60 g (2 oz) unsalted butter
1 large egg, beaten
170 g (6 oz) icing sugar, sifted

Mary's Tip
You have reached a soft dropping consistency when the mixture just drops off the spoon.

1. Preheat the oven to 180°C/360°F/gas 4 and grease and line an 18 × 28 cm (7 × 11 inch) shallow baking tin.

2. For the brownie, place the butter and chocolate together in a bowl over a saucepan of barely simmering water and leave until melted. Remove from the heat and stir in the sugar. Leave to cool.

3. Sift the flour and the salt into a mixing bowl. Make a well in the centre and pour in the cooled chocolate mixture. Mix together well.

4. Beat in the eggs and walnuts and stir in sufficient milk to give a soft dropping consistency. Pour the mixture into the tin, spread evenly and bake on the middle shelf for 30–40 minutes. Leave to cool in the tin.

5. For the topping, melt the chocolate and butter in a pan over saucepan of barely simmering water, stirring occasionally. Stir in the egg, remove from the heat and stir in the icing sugar. Beat well. Leave to cool slightly until the mixture thickens.

6. Place the base onto a wire tray then spread on the topping with a palette knife. Cut into squares.

～◦⌒ Almond and Mincemeat ◦⌒～ Fingers

This is a perfect way of using up leftover mincemeat from Christmas. If you're not keen on mincemeat, why not use 450 g (1 lb) cooked apples with 60 g (2 oz) sultanas instead.

Makes 14

For the base:

85 g (3 oz) butter
85 g (3 oz) caster sugar
1 large egg, separated
2 drops almond essence
170 g (6 oz) plain flour
85 g (3 oz) ground almonds

For the filling:

225 g (8 oz) mincemeat
grated rind of 1 small lemon

For the topping:

30 g (1 oz) flaked almonds

1. Preheat the oven to 180°C/360°F/gas 4 and grease an 18 × 28 cm (7 × 11 inch) shallow baking tin.

2. Place the butter and sugar into a bowl along with the egg yolk and the almond essence then mix to form a smooth paste. Work in most of the egg white, reserving 1 tsp.

3. Mix together the flour and ground almonds then add to the mixture. Mix until a smooth pastry is formed.

4. Divide the pastry in half, roll out and press into the base of the tin. Spread the mincemeat on top and then the grated lemon rind.

5. Roll out the remaining pastry and lightly press onto the top of the mincemeat filling. Brush with the remaining egg white and sprinkle on the flaked almonds. Leave in a cool place for 30 minutes. Mark into 14 fingers then bake on the middle shelf for approximately 20 minutes. After baking gently lift out the fingers onto a wire tray to cool.

❀ *Cheese Tray Bake* ❀

This delicious cheese tray bake makes an ideal dessert, served hot or cold with strawberries or other fruits.

Makes 18

For the base and topping:

285 g (10 oz) light brown soft sugar
340 g (12 oz) plain flour
170 g (6 oz) butter, melted

For the filling:

400 g (14 oz) cream cheese
60 g (2 oz) golden syrup
225 g (8 oz) caster sugar
2 large eggs, beaten
2 tbsp lemon juice
4 tbsp milk
1 tsp vanilla essence

Mary's Tip
Be very careful when you remove the tray bake from the tin – it is best left to cool completely before you take it out.

1. Preheat the oven to 180°C/360°F/gas 4 and grease an 18 × 28 cm (7 × 11 inch) shallow baking tin.

2. For the base and topping, combine the sugar and flour in a large bowl. Stir in the melted butter until the mixture resembles breadcrumbs. Fill the tin with two thirds of the mixture then press down evenly and firmly. Bake on the middle shelf for 20 minutes.

3. For the filling, beat the cream cheese, syrup and caster sugar until smooth. Beat in the egg, lemon juice, milk and vanilla essence.

4. After the base has cooked, remove from the oven and leave for 2 minutes then pour on the creamed filling. Return to the oven for 10 minutes. Carefully remove the tin from the oven and sprinkle on the remaining crumb-like, base mixture and bake for a final 20 minutes. Leave to cool in the tin, then cut into fingers.

FOR KIDS

~ఎ⦿

It is good to get children baking from an early age. You can start off by having them help you around the kitchen – you'll be amazed at what they pick up – and gradually they will learn to bake alone. There are plenty of child-friendly recipes in this section to help get them started.

~ఎ Gingerbread Biscuits ఎ~

A perennial favourite, these spicy treats can be cut into a range of shapes and sizes. And you can have lots of fun with decorating them, too.

For the gingerbread:

170 ml (6 fl oz) double cream
225 g (8 oz) light brown soft sugar
225 g (8 oz) black treacle
2 tsp ground ginger
grated rind of 1 lemon
2 tsp bicarbonate of soda
570g (1¼ lb) plain flour, sifted

For decoration:

royal icing
a variety of sweets

Mary's Tip

When decorating your gingerbread, use contrasting colour royal icing to secure pieces and then pipe over the edges to neaten if making a house; if you decide to make the classic gingerbread man, the eyes on the figure can be indented before baking.

1. Preheat the oven to 180°C/360°F/gas 4 and grease two or three baking trays, depending on their size.

2. Whisk the cream until it thickens slightly, then stir in the sugar, treacle, ginger, lemon rind and bicarbonate of soda and mix well together. Immediately sift the flour into the mixture and gradually stir in.

3. Continue working in the flour until a smooth, pliable dough is formed. Roll out onto a lightly floured surface and cut the pieces required.

4. Carefully place the gingerbread onto the trays, being careful not to distort the shapes, then brush with water and bake on the middle shelf for approximately 20–25 minutes, depending on the thickness of the biscuit. Remove from the trays to cool, then decorate as desired.

～ Chocolate Crackles ～

Wonderfully simple to make, these delicious chocolatey treats are a great starting point for budding, pint-sized bakers.

Makes 20

60 g (2 oz) plain or milk chocolate
60 g (2 oz) butter
60 g (2 oz) golden syrup
60 g (2 oz) caster sugar
45 g (1½ oz) puffed rice cereal

1. Melt the chocolate over a saucepan of barely simmering water.

2. In a separate saucepan, melt the butter, golden syrup and caster sugar over a low heat. Remove from the heat and add the chocolate to the pan.

3. Gently stir in the cereal until well blended. Place spoonfuls of the mixture into paper cases and leave until set.

⤺ *Christmas Cookies* ⤻

A simple recipe turned fun with the use of festive-shaped biscuit cutters. Feel free to use whichever shapes you come across, and why not try wrapping the finished cookies in coloured foil to hang on the Christmas tree.

Makes 30

115 g (4 oz) butter
145 g (5 oz) caster sugar
225 g (8 oz) plain flour, sifted
3 tbsp milk
1 tbsp golden syrup
Royal icing to decorate
Plain or milk chocolate, melted, to decorate

1. Preheat the oven to 190°C/375°F/gas 5 and grease two or three baking trays, depending on their size.

2. Place the butter, sugar, sifted flour, milk and syrup into a bowl and mix together using a spoon or electric beater until it forms a soft dough.

3. Turn out onto a lightly floured surface and knead. Gently roll out the dough and cut shapes as required.

4. Place onto the trays and bake on the middle shelf for 15 minutes or until pale gold in colour.

Mary's Tip
Do not over knead the dough as this will make the biscuits tough.

SAVOURY

~◦◦~

This book wouldn't be complete without a brief foray into the world of savoury snacks.

~◦◦~ Digestives ~◦◦~

A classic and versatile biscuit that tastes excellent served with cheese. For a sweet version, coat one side of the finished biscuit with melted chocolate.

Makes 16

100 g (3½ oz) wholemeal flour
45 g (1½ oz) fine or medium oatmeal
½ tsp baking powder
a pinch of salt
60 g (2 oz) butter
1 tbsp dark brown soft sugar
2–3 tbsp milk

1. Preheat the oven to 180°C/360°F/gas 4 and grease two or three baking trays, depending on their size.

2. Thoroughly mix the flour, oatmeal, baking powder and salt in a bowl. Rub in the butter until the mixture resembles breadcrumbs. Stir in the sugar and milk using the blade of a knife. Combine together then knead lightly to form a dough.

3. Roll out the dough on a floured surface to 3 mm (⅛ inch) thick. Cut out rounds using the mouth of a glass beaker (or something similar) and place onto the trays. Prick each biscuit with a fork and bake on the middle shelf for 12–15 minutes or until just browning on the edges. Lift the biscuits onto a wire tray to cool.

~ଊଵ~ *Cheese Biscuits* ~ଊଵ~

In order to get maximum taste from these delicious treats use a strong flavoured cheese.

Makes 14

60 g (2 oz) ready salted potato crisps
100 g (3½ oz) mature cheddar cheese, grated
70 g (2½ oz) plain flour, sifted
1 tsp icing sugar, sifted
¼ tsp mustard powder, sifted
a pinch of cayenne pepper, sifted
70 g (2½ oz) butter

1. Preheat the oven to 190°C/375°F/gas 5 and grease two or three baking trays, depending on their size.

2. Lightly crush the potato crisps and mix into a bowl with the cheese. Sift together the flour, icing sugar, mustard powder and cayenne pepper and stir into the cheese mixture. Melt the butter and stir into the mixture until well blended.

3. Divide the mixture into 14 pieces and place onto the trays in small heaps. Bake on the middle shelf for approximately 15 minutes or until golden brown. Leave on the trays for 3–4 minutes then place on a wire tray to cool.

~ঞ~ *Bacon and Cheese Ovals* ~ঞ~

Cheese, bacon and cayenne pepper come together beautifully in these scrumptious biscuits. They make an excellent base for hors d'oevres.

Makes 24

For the biscuits:

2 rashers back bacon
a little oil for frying
115 g (4 oz) plain wholemeal flour
¼ tsp ground coriander
a good pinch of cayenne pepper
85 g (3 oz) butter
85 g (3 oz) mature cheddar cheese, grated
1 tbsp golden syrup
3–4 tsp milk
milk for glazing

For the topping:

sesame seeds
poppy seeds
parmesan cheese, grated

1. Preheat the oven to 190°C/375°F/gas 5 and grease two or three baking trays, depending on their size.

2. Remove the rind from the bacon, cut into pieces and fry until very crisp. Drain on kitchen paper. Sift the flour, coriander and cayenne pepper together then mix in the butter, forming a crumb texture.

3. Chop the bacon finely then add to the mixture with the cheese and the golden syrup. Mix together to form a pliable dough, adding sufficient milk as required.

4. Roll out the dough on a surface dusted with wholemeal flour. Cut into fluted ovals and place onto trays. Brush with milk, sprinkle on various toppings and bake on the middle shelf for 10 minutes or until lightly browned.

Mary's Tip

Try experimenting with other savoury toppings, such as anchovies or chopped roasted peppers.

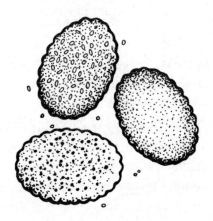

⊶ Curry Twists ⊶

These spiced treats make perfect dinner-party nibbles.

Makes 48

For the twists:

85 g (3 oz) wholemeal self-raising flour
85 g (3 oz) self-raising flour, sifted
a pinch of salt
1 tsp curry powder
115 g (4 oz) butter
1 tsp dark brown soft sugar
1 tbsp sesame seeds
1 egg yolk
1–2 tbsp milk

For the topping:

milk to glaze
1–2 tbsp sesame seeds

1. Preheat the oven to 190°C/375°F/gas 5 and grease two or three baking trays, depending on their size.

2. Place both flours, the salt and curry powder in a bowl, then rub in the butter until the mixture resembles breadcrumbs. Stir in the brown sugar and sesame seeds.

3. Mix in the egg yolk and sufficient milk to make a fairly soft, pliable dough. Roll out onto a lightly floured surface and cut into narrow strips, carefully twisting each strip one at a time.

4. Place onto the trays, brush with milk then sprinkle with sesame seeds. Bake on the middle shelf for 15 minutes or until golden brown. Leave on the trays to cool slightly before placing onto wire trays.

~◦~ *Savoury Whirls* ~◦~

These pretty little biscuits are packed full of flavour.

For the whirls:

115 g (4 oz) butter
1 tsp light brown soft sugar
145 g (5 oz) plain flour
large pinch each of salt, pepper and paprika
1 tbsp sesame seeds
2 tbsp parmesan cheese, grated
a little milk (optional)

For decoration:

a handful of parmesan cheese, grated
a handful of walnut pieces

1. Preheat the oven to 190°C/375°F/gas 5 and grease two or three baking trays, depending on their size.

2. Cream the butter and sugar until soft.

3. In a separate bowl, sift the flour, salt, pepper and paprika together then mix in the sesame seeds and cheese. Gradually work the dry ingredients into the creamed mixture to form a medium, soft dough. Mix in a few drops of milk if it is too stiff.

4. Place the mixture inside a piping bag fixed with a star-shaped nozzle and pipe rosettes onto the prepared tins. Sprinkle with grated cheese then place walnut pieces on top of each. Bake on the middle shelf for approximately 15 minutes.

INDEX

INDEX